INTEGRATING AND SUSTAINING HABITS OF MIND

SERIES FOREWORD: THINKING ON THE ROAD OF LIFE

DAVID PERKINS

While driving into town a few years ago, I found myself behind a young man in a red convertible. Like many people, I have certain expectations about young men in red convertibles, but this young man surprised me. When we reached a railroad crossing, he was painfully careful. He slowed down as he approached the tracks. The closer he got to the tracks, the more he slowed. As his car passed over the tracks, it hardly was moving at all. At this point, with great care, the young man looked to the left, and then he looked to the right. No train was coming. Satisfied with his safety, he gunned the engine and sped off. The young man was careful—and yet he wasn't! Surely, the middle of the tracks isn't the best position from which to scan for oncoming trains!

This man's behavior provides a kind of a metaphor for the mission of the four-book series Habits of Mind: A Developmental Series. When on the road of life, we ought to be thoughtful about what we are doing. For example, we ought to manage impulsivity and strive for accuracy, two of the worthwhile habits of mind this series describes. Yet if good thinking is to help us out in life, it has to go on the road with us. The trouble is, good thinking often gets left behind altogether, or it's exercised in flawed ways that don't do the job, as this young man demonstrated.

How can we encourage ourselves and others—particularly students—to take good thinking on the road? Habits of Mind: A Developmental Series explores one answer to that challenge: the cultivation of habits of mind, or habits of thought as John Dewey (1933) called them. The idea is that we should have habits of mind such as persistence and flexible thinking, just as we have habits like brushing our teeth or putting the dog out or being kind to people. Habits are not behaviors we pick up and lay down whimsically or arbitrarily. They are behaviors we exhibit reliably on appropriate occasions, and they are smoothly triggered without painstaking attention.

The very notion of habits of mind, however, poses a conceptual puzzle. By definition, habits are routine, but good use of the mind is not. The phrase habits of mind makes for a kind of oxymoron, like "loud silence" or "safe risk." Indeed, the story of the young man in the convertible illustrates what can go wrong with cultivating habits of mind. Here you have a habit of mind (being careful) played out in a way that misses the point (the man looks for the train from the middle of the tracks!). The very automaticity of a habit can undermine its function. Habits like that don't serve us well on a literal highway—or on the metaphorical road of life, either.

Can one have a habit of mind that truly does its work? The resolution to this puzzle is not very difficult. There's a difference between the thinking required to manage a mental process and the thinking done by the process. A habitual mental process does not require a lot of management to launch and sustain it, but that process itself may conduct mindful thinking. It may involve careful examination of alternatives, assessment of risks and consequences, alertness to error, and so on. For example, I have a simple, well-entrenched habit for the road of life: looking carefully when I depart a setting to be sure that I'm not leaving anything behind. This habit triggers and runs off reliably, with very little need for mindful management. But the behaviors deployed by the habit are highly mindful: scrutinizing the setting, glancing under chairs for concealed objects, and peering into drawers and closets for overlooked items.

In all fairness, the man in the convertible displayed a habit with something of this quality, too. It was good that he looked both ways with care. No doubt his scan of the tracks was precise and sensitive. He certainly would have detected any oncoming train. The difficulty was that his habit included a bug, rather like a bug in a computer program. Although his habit had a thoughtful phase (scanning the tracks), he was not thoughtful about his habit (choosing the point where he should scan the tracks).

Thus, the idea of habits of mind is not self-contradictory. A behavior can be habitual in its management but mindful in what it does. Still, one might ask, "Why not have it all? Ideally, shouldn't thinking processes be mindfully managed, mindful through and through for that extra edge?" Probably not! At least three things are wrong with this intuitively appealing ideal.

First, having to manage a thinking process mindfully would likely reduce the thoughtfulness of the process itself. As Herbert Simon (1957) and many other psychologists have emphasized, we humans have a limited capacity for processing information. Committing the management of a thinking process to routine is one way to open up mental space for the work the process has to do. Second, life has many distractions and preoccupations. A well-developed habit is more likely to make its presence felt than a practice that always must be deployed with meticulous deliberateness.

The third objection to this ideal of thoroughly mindful thinking goes beyond these pragmatic considerations to a logical point. Suppose the general rule is that thinking processes need mindful management. Surely managing a thinking process is itself a thinking process, so that process, too, needs mindful management. And the process of managing needs mindful management, and so on. It is mindful management all the way up, an infinite tower of metacognition, each process managed by its own mindfully managed manager. Clearly this approach won't work. Enter habits of mind, an apt challenge to a misguided conception of thinking as thoroughly thoughtful.

The notion of habits of mind also challenges another conception: the notion of intelligence. Most of the research on human intelligence is emphatically "abilities centric" (Perkins, Jay, & Tishman, 1993; Perkins, 1995). As mentioned in Chapter 1 of Book 1, the IQ tradition sees intelligence as a pervasive, monolithic mental ability, summed up by IQ and Charles Spearman's (1904) "g" factor, a statistical construct representing general intelligence. A number of theorists have proposed that there are many kinds of mental ability (two to 150, according to one model developed by Guilford [1967]). Although this book is not a setting where these models bear review (see Perkins, 1995), most of these models have something in common: They treat intelligence as an "ability on demand." Intelligence becomes a matter of what you can do when you know what it is that you're supposed to try to do (such as complete this analogy, decide whether this inference is warranted, or find the best definition for this word).

Thinking in much of life is a different matter. In daily life, we not only have to solve problems, we also have to find them amid an ongoing, complex stream of stimuli imposing constant demands and distractions. On the road of life, our thinking is not just a matter of the thinking we can do when we know a peak performance is demanded. It also is a matter of our sensitivity to occasions and our inclination to invest ourselves in them thoughtfully. High mental ability alone may serve us well when we're sitting at a desk, our pencils poised, but good habits of mind keep us going in the rest of the world. This point is underscored by scholars such as philosopher Robert Ennis (1986), with his analysis of critical thinking dispositions; psychologist Jonathan Baron (1985), with his dispositional model of intelligence; and psychologist Ellen Langer (1989), with her conception of mindfulness.

A program of empirical research on thinking dispositions, which my colleague Shari Tishman and I have directed over the past several years, underscores what's at stake here (e.g., Perkins & Tishman, 1997). Working with students from middle to late elementary school, we investigated their performance on a variety of critical and creative thinking tasks involving narratives. Over and over again, we found that they could do far better than they did do when they explored options, considered pros and cons, and performed similar tasks. Their performance was limited because they often did not detect when such moves were called for. When they did detect what they should do, or when the places were pointed out, they easily could show the kind of thinking called for. They didn't lack intelligence in the sense of ability on demand, but they lacked the habits of mind that provide for ongoing alertness to shortfalls in thinking.

In that spirit, this series of four books speaks not just to intelligence in the laboratory but also to intelligent behavior in the real world. It addresses how we can help youngsters get ready for the road of life, a sort of "drivers' education" for the mind. Imagine what life would be like without good habits of various sorts. Our teeth would rot, our bodies collapse, our gardens wither, our tempers sour, and our friends drift away. We do better to the extent that we get direction from good habits, including habits of mind. When today's students hit the road, the ideas in Habits of Mind: A Developmental Series can help them ride on smooth mental wheels, checking for trains *before* they start over the tracks!

REFERENCES

Baron, J. (1985). *Rationality and intelligence*. New York: Cambridge University Press.

Dewey, J. (1933). *How we think: A restatement of the relation of reflective thinking to the education process*. New York: D. C. Heath.

Ennis, R. H. (1986). A taxonomy of critical thinking dispositions and abilities. In J. B. Baron & R. S. Sternberg (Eds.), *Teaching thinking skills: Theory and practice* (pp. 9–26). New York: W. H. Freeman.

Guilford, J. P. (1967). *The nature of human intelligence*. New York: McGraw-Hill.

Langer, E. J. (1989). *Mindfulness*. Reading, MA: Addison-Wesley.

Perkins, D. N. (1995). *Outsmarting IQ: The emerging science of learnable intelligence.* New York: The Free Press.

Perkins, D. N., Jay, E., & Tishman, S. (1993). Beyond abilities: A dispositional theory of thinking. *The Merrill-Palmer Quarterly, 39*(1), 1–21.

Perkins, D. N., & Tishman, S. (1997). *Dispositional aspects of intelligence.* Paper presented at the Second Spearman Seminar, The University of Plymouth, Devon, England.

Simon, H. A. (1957). *Models of man: Social and rational.* New York: Wiley.

Spearman, C. (1904). General intelligence, objectively defined and measured. *American Journal of Psychology, 15,* 201–209.

PREFACE TO THE SERIES

ARTHUR L. COSTA AND BENA KALLICK

D onna Norton Swindal, a resource teacher in Burnsville, Minnesota, recently shared an interesting story about a 4th grader who brought a newspaper clipping to class. The article described genocide in a troubled African country. After a lively discussion about what was happening there, one concerned classmate stated, "If those people would just learn to persist, they could solve their problems."

His philosophical colleague added, "If they would learn to listen with understanding and empathy, they wouldn't have this problem."

Yet another activist suggested, "We need to go over there and teach them the habits of mind!"

What are the "habits of mind" these concerned young citizens were so eager to share? They are the overarching theme of Habits of Mind: A Developmental Series, and they are the heart of the book you now hold in your hands.

THE BEGINNING

The ideas in Habits of Mind: A Developmental Series first started in 1982. Our beginning conversations about Intelligent Behaviors flourished into rich experiments with classroom practitioners until finally we arrived at this juncture: a series of four books to inspire the work of others. In our daily work with students and staff, we discovered that names were needed for the behaviors that would be expected from one another if, indeed, we were living in a productive learning organization. We came to call these dispositions "habits of mind," indicating that the behaviors require a discipline of the mind that is practiced so it becomes a habitual way of working toward more thoughtful, intelligent action.

The intent of Habits of Mind: A Developmental Series is to help educators teach toward these habits of mind, which we see as broad, enduring, and essential lifespan learnings that are as appropriate for adults as they are for students. Our hope is that by teaching students (and adults) the habits of mind, students will be more disposed to draw upon the habits when they are faced with uncertain or challenging situations. And, ultimately, we hope the habits will help educators develop thoughtful, compassionate, and cooperative human beings who can live productively in an increasingly chaotic, complex, and information-rich world (as the 4th graders above so aptly demonstrated!).

THE HABITS OF MIND

The following list contains the habits of mind described in Habits of Mind: A Developmental Series. The habits begin with the individual and move out to the entire community. Keep in mind, however, that the list is not complete. As our conversations continue—as you work with the habits, too—we all will likely identify other habits that should be added to this list.

The 16 habits of mind we have identified are

- Persisting
- Managing impulsivity
- Listening with understanding and empathy
- Thinking flexibly
- Thinking about thinking (metacognition)
- Striving for accuracy
- Questioning and posing problems
- Applying past knowledge to new situations
- Thinking and communicating with clarity and precision
- Gathering data through all senses
- Creating, imagining, innovating
- Responding with wonderment and awe
- Taking responsible risks
- Finding humor
- Thinking interdependently
- Remaining open to continuous learning

The most powerful communities use these habits of mind to guide all their work. Yet sometimes the practicality of school life requires that people make individual commitments with the hope that their beliefs and behaviors will affect the whole. Teaching with the habits of mind requires a shift toward a broader conception of educational outcomes and how they are cultivated, assessed, and communicated. Taken together, the four books in Habits of Mind: A Developmental Series aim to help you work toward and achieve these goals.

A DUAL PURPOSE

In this four-book series, we provide

- Descriptions and examples of the habits of mind.
- Instructional strategies intended to foster acquisition of these habits at school and at home.
- Assessment tools that provide a means of gathering evidence of student growth in the habits of mind.
- Ways of involving students, teachers, and parents in communicating progress toward acquiring the habits of mind.
- Descriptions from schools, teachers, and administrators about how they have incorporated the habits of mind and the effects of their work.

Our true intent for these books, however, is far more panoramic, pervasive, and long-range. Each book in the series works at two levels. The first level encompasses immediate and practical considerations that promote using the habits of mind in classrooms and schools every day. The second level addresses a larger, more elevated concern for creating a learning culture that considers habits of mind as central to building a thoughtful community. We summarize these levels as follows.

BOOK 1: *DISCOVERING AND EXPLORING HABITS OF MIND*

Level 1: Defining the habits of mind and understanding the significance of developing these habits as a part of lifelong learning.

Level 2: Encouraging schools and communities to elevate their level and broaden their scope of curricular outcomes by focusing on more essential, enduring lifespan learnings.

BOOK 2: *ACTIVATING AND ENGAGING HABITS OF MIND*

Level 1: Learning how to teach the habits directly and to reinforce them throughout the curriculum.

Level 2: Enhancing instructional decision making to employ content not as an end of instruction but as a vehicle for activating and engaging the mind.

BOOK 3: *ASSESSING AND REPORTING ON HABITS OF MIND*

Level 1: Learning about a range of techniques and strategies for gathering evidence of students' growth in and performance of the habits of mind.

Level 2: Using feedback to guide students to become self-assessing and to help school teams and parents use assessment data to cultivate a more thoughtful culture.

BOOK 4: *INTEGRATING AND SUSTAINING HABITS OF MIND*

Level 1: Learning strategies for extending the impact of habits of mind throughout the school community.

Level 2: Forging a common vision among all members of the educational community from kindergarten through post-graduate work: teachers, administrative teams, administrators, librarians, staff developers, teacher educators, school board members, and parents. This vision describes the characteristics of efficacious and creative thinkers and problem solvers.

In teaching for the habits of mind, we are interested in not only how many answers students know but also how students behave when they don't know an answer. We are interested in observing how students produce knowledge rather than how they merely reproduce it. A critical attribute of intelligent human beings is not only having information but also knowing how to act on it.

By definition, a problem is any stimulus, question, task, phenomenon, or discrepancy, the explanation for which is not immediately known. Intelligent behavior is performed in response to such questions and problems. Thus, we are interested in focusing on student performance under those challenging conditions—dichotomies, dilemmas, paradoxes, ambiguities and enigmas—that demand strategic reasoning, insightfulness, perseverance, creativity, and craftsmanship to resolve them.

Teaching toward the habits of mind is a team effort. Because repeated opportunities over a long period are needed to acquire these habits of mind, the entire staff must dedicate itself to teaching toward, recognizing, reinforcing, discussing, reflecting on, and assessing the habits of mind. When students encounter these habits at each grade level in the elementary years and in each classroom throughout the secondary day—and when the habits also are reinforced and modeled at home—they become internalized, generalized, and habituated.

We need to find new ways of assessing and reporting growth in the habits of mind. We cannot measure process-oriented outcomes using old-fashioned, product-oriented assessment techniques. Gathering evidence of performance and growth in the habits of mind requires "kid watching." As students interact with real-life, day-to-day problems in school, at home, on the playground, alone, and with friends, teaching teams and other adults can collect anecdotes and examples of written and visual expressions that reveal students' increasingly voluntary and spontaneous use of these habits of mind. This work also takes time. The habits are never fully mastered, though they do become increasingly apparent over time and with repeated experiences and opportunities to practice and reflect on their performance.

Considered individually, each book helps you start down a path that will lead to enhanced curriculum, instruction, and assessment practices. Taken together, the books in Habits of Mind: A Developmental Series provide a road map for individuals, for classrooms, and ultimately for a full-system approach. For our purposes, we think a "system" is approached when the habits of mind are integrated throughout the culture of the organization. That is, when all individual members of a learning community share a common vision of the attributes of effective and creative problem solvers, when resources are allocated to the development of those dispositions; when strategies to enhance those characteristics in themselves and others are planned, and when members of the organization join in efforts to continuously assess, refine, and integrate those behaviors in their own and the organization's practices.

> *I can tell you right now that we will never be able to forget the habits of mind. They helped us so much! They taught us better ways of doing things and how to resolve problems! We learned respect and manners. My mother was so very impressed with this teaching. Also we learned that you need to get along with others and not to disrespect them either.*
>
> Excerpted from a 5th grader's
> valedictorian address upon graduation from
> Friendship Valley Elementary School, Westminster, Maryland

PREFACE TO BOOK 4

ARTHUR L. COSTA AND BENA KALLICK

In the first three volumes of Habits of Mind: A Developmental Series, we described 16 habits of mind (Book 1), presented strategies for activating and engaging those habits (Book 2), and introduced techniques for assessing them (Book 3). Our intent was to help schools and districts put the habits in place so that staff members would spontaneously ask themselves questions such as these when confronted with conflicts, tensions, dilemmas, and other ambiguous situations:

- What is the most flexible thing I can do in this situation?
- How might this situation be viewed from the other person's perspective?
- What powerful questions can I ask to gain clarity and more information about this problem?
- What might I carry forth from this situation that will help me solve future problems of this type?
- What are some creative, innovative approaches to solving this problem?

In the second and third books of the series, we described how teachers can use the habits of mind as they make daily decisions about curriculum, instruction, and assessment. We wanted teachers to form images of themselves as facilitators of these habits of mind in others. Thus, they would ask themselves questions such as these:

- How can I use the content of this lesson to help my students experience one or more of the habits of mind?
- What can I look for in my students' behavior over time as indicators that they are habituating the habits of mind?
- How can I help students become aware of these habits of mind in their own and others' behaviors?

• How can I invite students to consciously use the habits of mind as they approach projects and learning activities in this class?
• How am I modeling these habits of mind in my own behavior?

We believe that teachers will be more likely to teach these habits of mind if these same values, dispositions, and characteristics are reflected in the policies, procedures, and practices of the school, district, and community. Therefore, Book 4 describes how organizations can integrate the habits of mind into the culture and daily life of the school. As groups, communities, staffs, departments, grade-level teams, school faculties, and school districts confront their work, they also encounter enigmas, dilemmas, and ambiguous situations. We want Book 4 to help all these learning organizations use the habits of mind as they ask themselves questions such as these:

• What can we learn from resolving this problem? How might it contribute to our expanding reservoir of knowledge?
• How can the resolution to this problem strengthen our learning community?
• How can we become more flexible, empathic, and appreciative of diversity as a result of working on this problem?
• What essential questions should we ask ourselves and others to help resolve this problem?
• What strategies can we use to document our growth and learning as an organization?

Chapter 1 describes an organization's role in furthering the habits of mind. It provides an introduction to seven indicators that can guide schools working to become "homes for the mind." These indicators are rooted in a model described by Malcolm Baldrige, who is well known for his work with quality and excellence in the business community. We recommend that an organization assess itself using these seven indicators as the criteria for staff work. (The list of indicators is defined more fully in the Appendix.)

In Chapter 2, we elaborate on the seven indicators as we describe our vision of a school that is a home for the mind. We describe how the habits of mind serve not only as the centerpiece for curriculum, but also as building blocks of a school's culture and community. Theory alone is not enough. Demonstrating theory in action and developing benchmarks unite the indicators with practice.

Chapters 3 and 4 look at infusing the habits of mind into a school or district culture. In Chapter 3, Curtis Schnorr and Thommie DePinto

Piercy describe one school's learning journey toward achieving its vision of a home for the mind. When Friendship Valley Elementary School in Westminster, Maryland, was first built, Schnorr served as principal and Piercy was vice-principal. They describe the construction of the new school's culture: a place where the values, recognitions, celebrations, assessments, and behaviors of all the stakeholders are congruent with the habits of mind. This culture was not achieved in a few easy steps; establishing the culture took time, leadership, resources, and, of course, persistence. In Chapter 4, Deborah Hansen, coordinator of staff development at DeLong Middle School in the Eau Claire Area School District in Eau Claire, Wisconsin, describes the learning journey she and her colleagues took as they infused the habits of mind into their district's culture.

We are often asked questions about how to achieve the seven indicators described in Chapters 1, 2, and the Appendix. We, as authors, can offer answers, but we believe educators gain even more by tapping into the experiences of practitioners who have implemented the habits of mind. Thus, in Chapter 5, we have drawn from the learning journeys of several individuals, schools, and districts to share a wealth of knowledge and experience related to the habits of mind. We have organized this information around key questions related to the indicators introduced in Chapter 1.

Once a school or district adopts and implements the habits of mind, the task is still not complete. Leaders must persistently maintain their focus on the habits even as they are buffeted by special-interest groups, politicians, or state departments of education. Chapter 6 describes how schools can stay the course and develop the habits of mind for a continuously improving society.

We close this book with Chapter 7, a list of strategies for bringing the habits of mind to life in your school, district, or community. The list is purposely incomplete, and we invite you and your colleagues to brainstorm additions, prioritize the habits, and develop action plans for their implementation.

From the Editors: Throughout the book, student names are fictitious.

BUILDING LEARNING ORGANIZATIONS

ARTHUR L. COSTA AND BENA KALLICK

To thrive in the 21st century, schools must become adaptive organizations capable of continuous learning, growth, and change. We make this statement because of the incredible amount of information now available to help educators refine and improve their work in all areas of curriculum, instruction, administration, and parent and community relations. Much of this same information was available in the past, but technology has fundamentally changed information management. Schools need new organizational habits to take advantage of the wealth of data that technology makes so rapidly available.

Successful learning organizations continually collect, analyze, and learn from data, and they self-modify on the basis of what they have learned. They generate and gather these data from a variety of sources, and they use the data to seek even more information. Learning organizations study innovative practices, but they also continuously examine the costs and benefits of such change, weighing these factors against the results of students' performance on both internal and external measures.

In the early '90s, businesses called this kind of reflection and modification "reengineering." Companies discovered the significance of examining *process* to improve the quality and productivity of their work (Hammer & Champy, 1993). Soon, total quality management (TQM) became a popular, catch-all descriptor for the process of examining and attending to systematic measures of progress.

Educators adapted many of these business practices, calling the concepts and principles "restructuring" and "outcome-based education" (Bonstingl, 1992). About the same time, schools also began to feel the effects of a world in which technology made organizational learning more efficient. In this early romance with technology, many districts focused more on hardware and software than on how to best use technology to achieve their goals. Eventually, schools realized that technology is only a tool that facilitates sharing organizational knowledge, improving decision making, thinking more effectively, and learning more efficiently.

Technology can help educators collect data, but humans need to talk about these data, make sense out of the information, search for patterns, and ultimately solve problems together. To take advantage of this kind of "internal school knowledge," we must rebuild the culture. Changing the culture means changing its habits. Many teachers already study student assessment data and student work, and they share information with colleagues about what happens to students from class to class and year to year. Those conversations, however, are limited by the amount of discipline and practice people have had in thoughtful, critical dialogue.

The habits of mind can guide groups away from a highly individual, personal approach to a social and collective understanding. As educators learn how to effectively practice the habits of mind, the school culture shifts from personal knowledge to shared knowledge. The school is no longer just a set of classrooms adjacent to one another; the school becomes a community of learners. Members of this school community—not technology—build the learning organization, and we believe the habits of mind should be the foundation of all their work.

FINDING THE KEY

If schools are to learn from their successes and failures, sharing information is key. Yet schools often face many barriers to sharing the kind of information that leads to organizational learning. Some barriers include lack of time, sparse opportunities to think with other teachers across grade levels and in other buildings, and the proprietary nature of the work of disciplines. Schools also find a variety of barriers in departments, individual teachers, and an unwritten code that says examining practice threatens teachers' evaluations.

To promote a learning atmosphere, adults themselves must learn how to use the habits of mind to support sharing. Teachers, administrators, and other school personnel must be able to practice the habits of questioning and posing problems, thinking flexibly, and listening with understanding and empathy, to name just a few. Consider the chart in Figure 1.1. Does your school match the description of a pro-sharing culture or an anti-sharing culture, or is it somewhere in between? After you've spent some time considering your school, read through the following two examples. They describe how staff members in a high school and an elementary school shared information to resolve challenging questions about improving practice and better serving students.

FIGURE 1.1
Pro-Sharing Culture vs. Anti-Sharing Culture

Pro-Sharing Culture	Anti-Sharing Culture
Learning occurs through teaching and sharing. Systems and incentives support sharing information and insights.	No learning occurs through teaching and sharing. No systems or incentives promote sharing information and insights. Many incentives and systems work against sharing.
Reflection is purposeful and planned. Communal understanding is achieved through story telling.	Little time or attention for reflection is provided. Staff members feel they are constantly fighting the clock, so they don't take the time to identify lessons learned from projects.
New knowledge is continuously exchanged and created. As experimentation occurs, people share and learn.	Little or no new knowledge is exchanged or created. Assumptions about projects or activities go unchallenged.
Staff members share common areas of interest and expertise. Individuals are hired and promoted on the basis of technical expertise as well as their potential to contribute to the common vision and goals.	Staff members possessively guard their areas of interest and expertise. Individuals are hired and promoted mainly for their technical expertise.
Staff members openly discuss common challenges and problems. Sharing success *and* failure is part of the professional ethic.	Administrators and staff members are reluctant to talk about projects that did not work well. Sharing success is acceptable, but sharing failure is frowned upon.
Staff members share personal and professional relationships across grades, subjects, and departments, which promote shared knowledge.	The different missions and visions of grades, subjects, and departments produce different cultures. This environment inhibits personal and professional relationships and obstructs transfer of knowledge.

SHARING PROGRAMS AND PRACTICES

Teachers at Cherry Hill West High School in Cherry Hill, New Jersey, came together to consider how to help low-performing students meet the state's new, more rigorous standards. At their first meeting, teachers discussed the many practices that had already been developed for and used with these students. Rather than immediately invent another practice or program, they spent considerable time looking at what they could learn from their past efforts. They worked productively as a group, using the habit of mind applying past knowledge to new situations.

Once the teachers generated a list of programs and practices they'd already tried, they saw that their need was most likely to be met by experienced teachers who had already worked with the targeted students. Rather than assume the answer to their challenge lay elsewhere, they agreed that carefully researching their own work showed that an answer probably was already available in the school. They just didn't see the answer yet!

Throughout their conversations, the teachers listened with understanding and empathy as many frustrations were voiced. At the same time, they worked flexibly, trying to move away from past traditions that had not succeeded. Most important, they persisted with a focus on the significance of remaining open to continuous learning. Here is a summary of their work from one meeting:

Vision: The ultimate vision or direction for this project is to create a learning organization at Cherry Hill West. What that means is an organization that

- Uses standards as a means of establishing high expectations for all students.
- Uses assessment measures, both external as well as internal, as a way of guiding instruction and decisions for school change.
- Develops a structured way for teachers to share the knowledge from practice that works toward improving student learning, particularly focusing on the students who are in the remedial and modified group and using the habits of mind to guide the groups' dynamics.
- Develops a method for organizing time so that teachers can (1) exchange and learn from one another, (2) plan and collaborate on behalf of common practices or interdisciplinary practices or both, and (3) conference collaboratively with students they have in common, when necessary.

The work will be guided by a process that uses a feedback spiral for growth and learning.

At this point, group members decided to tap into the staff's extensive knowledge base. The teachers started to gather data, focusing on students in the remedial and modified programs. One of the group's greatest concerns was ensuring that this work was not greeted with cynicism and apathy. They decided that introducing the habits of mind to guide their group process could help them replace poor habits of mind related to communication and problem solving.

Instead of immediately jumping to find new solutions, the group dedicated itself to using the habits to create a more thoughtful process. They considered questions such as the following, which specifically tapped into the habits of mind:

• How do we envision successful students from the remedial and modified category whose learning can improve sufficiently so that they are able to meet the standards defined by the school? [Striving for accuracy; creating, imagining, innovating]
• How do we envision the teachers who will directly work with these students? What are the characteristics that teachers must develop to work successfully with these students? [Striving for accuracy; thinking and communicating with clarity and precision]
• What lessons have we learned from the many programs we have put in place to address these students? How can we ensure that we will learn from these lessons rather than repeat them? [Applying past knowledge to new situations; remaining open to continuous learning]

Next, the group developed a structure for sharing this knowledge. They created an electronic template for teachers to keep track of their practices. Then, they designed a database of successful practices, which all staff members could use. Though the database focuses on knowledge already in the school, the teachers are alert to new research and practices that they might want to add.

A feedback spiral is a useful way to summarize these teachers' learning and reflection (see Figure 1.2 on p. 6). The spiral encompasses these steps:

1. Clarify goals and purposes.
2. Plan.
3. Take action/Experiment.
4. Assess/Gather evidence.
5. Study, reflect, evaluate.
6. Modify actions based on new knowledge.
7. Revisit, clarify goals and purposes.
8. Begin the spiral again.

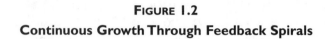

FIGURE 1.2
Continuous Growth Through Feedback Spirals

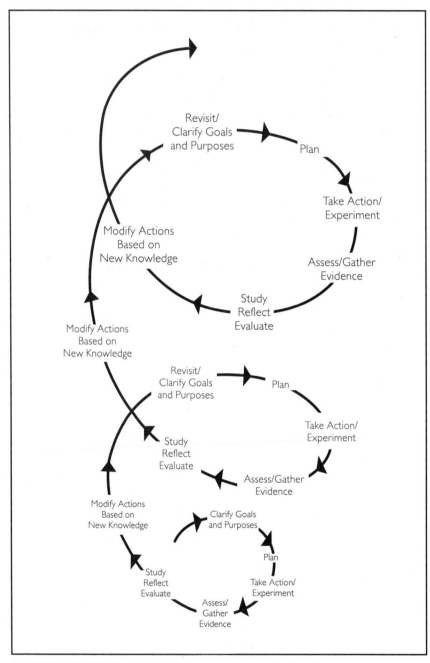

Source: Costa & Kallick, 1995, p. 27.

SHARING STUDENT DATA

Mamaroneck Avenue School in Mamaroneck, New York, faced the problem of increasing referrals for special services with no new resources to accommodate the increase. As a result, the special services staff grew frustrated, and they were concerned about the future of the children they served.

The principal called a meeting to address the issue, and with the guidance of a consultant, staff members voiced their feelings and concerns. Rather than dwell on these worries, group members quickly moved toward a problem-solving approach. They focused on listening to one another with understanding and empathy, and they purposely practiced thinking flexibly.

With some facilitation, staff members started to pose important questions: How many of us are dealing with the same child? Do we only know this by coincidence, or is there some record we can turn to? What do we know about the students we serve over time? Is there any record we can turn to that will tell us how successful students are once they leave our programs? Why can't we connect better with the classroom teacher, who needs to understand what we do in order to follow through with the child? What assessment data do we have in common?

These questions led the group to consider what data are needed to discover meaningful patterns. Individual specialists did most of the documentation and record keeping, so staff members had access to little collective knowledge about students. After much critical reflection, staff members agreed to take the following actions:

• Assess all kindergarten students at the end of the year using a combination of assessments from speech, reading, and special education. All teachers and administrators would help conduct the assessments. Thus, each person would have no more than six to eight children to assess.

• Enter the data from these assessments into a student record, designed with the help of a programmer. The team would determine the need for remediation. In September, identified students would receive special services.

• Open the student's record to all teachers to create a common place for sharing progress. Teachers would keep a careful record of what interventions were particularly successful for the child. All information would be put into this student record, and any teacher could access the information in the computer.

• Hold regular meetings to review students' data. Teachers committed to learn how to use the technology and how to analyze data for meaningful patterns. They also agreed to share practices that worked with particular students.

• Assess 1st grade students in January and then again in June. The main question would be, What worked for students, and to what degree?

This group made careful decisions about knowledge management. They seriously considered the potential for documenting practices and their results. They defined assessment as an ongoing process, and they decided to develop regular assessments as they worked with students. In addition, they committed to work together so that their dialogue about students was focused, shared, and documented.

These educators made the habits of mind explicit as they worked through the data. They practiced questioning and posing problems, applying past knowledge to new situations, listening with understanding and empathy, and managing impulsivity. In the end, the habits of mind helped their meetings become more efficient and more thoughtful. One of the most noticeable results was a significant change toward a culture for continuous learning. The school now plans to adopt the habits of mind for all members of their learning community.

SELF-ASSESSING SCHOOL PROGRESS

As schools develop a learning culture grounded in the habits of mind, they will want to gauge their progress. In keeping with the feedback spiral for continuous learning and growth (see Figure 1.2), we have designed a self-assessment tool (see Appendix) to help schools answer questions about their work. This tool is based on the model for continuous learning espoused by business leaders such as W. Edwards Deming, Tom Peters, and Malcolm Baldrige.

The concept of continuous improvement implies a cyclical movement as an organization progresses through answering three questions: (1) What *approach* are we taking? (2) To what degree do we see *implementation*? (3) What is the evidence of *results*?

Approach describes the process chosen to bring about the practice. Approach might also be called "theory." For example, consider a school district that decides to pursue inquiry-based learning. The district decides to provide inservice workshops for all teachers and to offer a variety of documents to guide teachers. Each of these steps would be considered the approach.

Implementation is the degree to which you see the approach in operation. Thus, this school district would seek information about the degree to which inquiry-based learning is actually happening in classrooms. Many districts find they score well on the approach: Documents are in place, teachers participate in the inservice workshops, and teachers seem to understand the how and why of the topic. Yet many times, the district finds little evidence of the practice in classrooms. Though understanding increases, practice does not always change.

Results are the evidence of an improvement in learning. The district described earlier would likely see little evidence of increased learning. This result is not surprising because there is little evidence of practice.

The value of breaking assessment into three components is that you have many ways to analyze information, as the school described demonstrates. For example,

• There is evidence of increased learning but no evidence of an approach. The question raised by such data is, How can we define the approach we are using so that we can make it explicit to the whole organization?

• There is evidence of strong approach and implementation but little evidence of results. The questions raised by such data are, Do we have the right approach? Do we have enough implementation to suggest results? Do we have the right assessments?

The Appendix details a set of seven indicators that can be used with this three-part model to self-assess your school. We developed these indicators with the assumption that you are working toward building a school as a home for the mind (see Chapter 2). The indicators are

• Shared vision, outcomes, and goals.
• Curriculum, instruction, and assessment.
• School culture.
• Communication and collaboration.
• Leadership.
• Resourceful school community.
• Continuous learning.

Note that the charts in the Appendix detailing these self-assessment indicators encompass several variables. First are the seven indicators themselves. Second are the three components of the self-assessment: approach, implementation, and results. Third are the categories for defining your type of school:

• *In the habit.* The behavior has become habituated throughout the organization. The behavior is a cultural norm and is performed spontaneously.

• *Practicing.* There are conscious and explicit procedures and strategies for focusing on, installing, and monitoring the behavior throughout the organization.

• *Aware.* There is an appreciation of the value of and an understanding of the need for the behavior.

The information in the Appendix is only a beginning. You probably will want to modify the descriptors in each part of the chart to reflect your school's situation. The data generated through this model do not imply that the approach you have taken is the right one. This model does not assume that the degree of implementation is necessarily the problem. The model pushes for results, but it does not ignore the thoughtful actions that must be in place to generate results. As the feedback spiral also suggests, continuous growth and learning require attention to all three elements: approach, implementation, and results. These seven indicators and the self-assessment model simply offer a method for gauging how you are doing in your spiraling journey of learning.

REFERENCES

Bonstingl, J. J. (1992). *Schools of quality: An introduction to total quality management in education.* Alexandria, VA: Association for Supervision and Curriculum Development.

Costa, A., & Kallick, B. (1995). *Assessment in the learning organization: Shifting the paradigm.* Alexandria, VA: Association for Supervision and Curriculum Development.

Hammer, M., & Champy, J. (1993). *Reengineering the corporation.* New York: Harper Business.

2

CONSTRUCTING A HOME
FOR THE MIND

ARTHUR L. COSTA AND BENA KALLICK

Visitors to the town of Pugwash in Nova Scotia, Canada, are greeted with this sign: "Welcome to PUGWASH, Home of the Thinkers." The city obviously is proud that it was the site of the first Pugwash Conference in 1957, which brought together 22 influential scientists to discuss the threat of thermonuclear weapons. Since then, a variety of scholars and government leaders have met at Pugwash Conferences around the world to consider issues related to armed conflict and global problems. The Pugwash Conferences and Joseph Rotblat, one of the group's founders, were awarded the 1995 Nobel Peace Prize.

"Home of the Thinkers" sends a bold message about what the community of Pugwash values. Their welcome sign could easily recognize the city's beautiful seaside setting, its summertime Gathering of the Clans Celebration, or its deep historical ties. Instead, Pugwash calls itself "Home of the Thinkers."

Many schools proclaim that they value the habits of mind above all else. By themselves, however, proclamations are empty. Schools can't just say they value the habits of mind and expect success. The habits must be lived and practiced by every individual in the learning organization, and they must be institutionalized throughout the entire system. If schools truly value the habits of mind, they must also deliberately construct homes for the mind.

FINDING "LEVERAGE POINTS"

Many factors influence teachers' thinking as they make their daily decisions about curriculum and instruction. Their own culture, content knowledge, cognitive style, knowledge about students, and professional values and beliefs influence their instructional judgment. Additionally, studies of the relationship of school context to teachers' work suggest that the interpersonal and structural conditions that characterize teachers' work will also affect the impact the teachers have on their students (Louis, Marks, & Kruse, 1996). Jack Frymier (1987), professor emeritus from The University of Ohio, believes that one factor overrides all others: "In the main, the bureaucratic structure of the workplace is more influential in determining what professionals do than are personal abilities, professional training, or previous experience. Therefore, change efforts should focus on the structure of the workplace, not the teachers" (p. 10).

Frymier suggests we can identify less obvious, but vastly more persuasive, influences on teacher thought: the norms, values, and culture of the school setting in which teachers work. The school environment radiates unseen but powerful cues. These cues signal an institutional value system that governs the operation of the organization (Saphier & King, 1985). Efforts to integrate the habits of mind will prove futile unless the school environment signals the staff, students, and community that developing and living the habits are the school's basic values.

Systems analysts believe in "leverage points," or places within a complex system where a small shift in one condition can produce significant changes throughout the entire system. In the remainder of this chapter, we will detail seven factors that can be leverage points for creating a home for the mind that embraces the habits of mind:

- Shared vision, outcomes, and goals.
- Curriculum, instruction, and assessment.
- School culture.
- Communication and collaboration.
- Leadership.
- Resourceful school community.
- Continuous learning.

SHARED VISION, OUTCOMES, AND GOALS

Autopoesis: (Greek) Self-production. The characteristic of living systems to continuously renew themselves and to regulate this process in such a way that the integrity of their structure is maintained. It is a natural process, which supports the quest for structure, process renewal, and integrity.

Margaret Wheatley, *Leadership and the New Science*

To ensure that all members of the school community are a part of creating the learning and knowledge, the school must clearly convey a vision of itself as a place for learning. For example, Encinal High School in Alameda, California, states its vision this way: "Encinal High School is a home for the active mind—a cooperative community promoting knowledge, self-understanding, mutual respect, global understanding, adaptability to change, and a love for lifelong learning."

Enhancing intelligent behavior is explicitly stated in this district's philosophy and mission. District goals, policies, and practices are constantly scrutinized for their consistency with and contribution to that philosophy. The district aligns its procedures for continuing to study, refine, and improve practices so that the school grows toward more intelligent application of the habits of mind.

Students, staff, and parents will better understand the importance of the habits of mind when the habits are overtly named as the purpose of education. Mottos, slogans, and mission statements should be placed prominently in all classrooms, schools, and district offices. For example, "Thought is Taught at Huntington Beach High" is emblazoned on one school's note pads. "Lincoln Schools are Thought-Full Schools" is the motto painted on one district's delivery trucks for all the community to see. "Make Thinking Happen" is printed on the stationery of another school we've visited.

CURRICULUM, INSTRUCTION, AND ASSESSMENT

Curriculum restructuring is the most critical—but least acknowledged—component of school reform. Unfortunately, current reform movements are being driven by national, state, and local mandates related to rescheduling of time segments during the school day or year, redistributing the power of decision-making processes, investing in technology, and recombining interdisciplinary teams and subjects (Cawelti, 1995). These and other such reforms constitute the *how* of delivery, not the substance of *what* is being delivered.

Curriculum is the pulse of the school. Curriculum can also be considered the currency by which teachers exchange thoughts and ideas with students and the broader school community. Curriculum is the vital element that binds the organization together. When we address the very heart of an organization—what it is that we want students to know and be able to do—then all other reform efforts will fall into place.

Shifting Mental Models

Michael Fullan (1993) observes that we need to take a "quantum leap" in how we think about and develop curriculum. For most people, though, a change in mental models implies the discomfort of the unknown: the psychologically unknown risks of a new venture, the physically unknown demands on time and energy, and the intellectually unknown requirements for new skills and knowledge. People who are invested in their present ways of working believe that if they can just do more of what they are currently doing, everything will improve.

Technology, however, has created an information-based society that requires a shift in the way we think about knowledge. We must reexamine what students need to know, making certain that we distinguish information (data and facts) from knowledge (conceptual understanding). We will also have to reexamine what we want students to be able to do. The habits of mind offer the disciplines of mind that are necessary to make sense out of the ever-increasing information and knowledge generated in today's technological society.

As educators adopt this new vision, some traditional views of education will be declared obsolete. Our perceptions of schools, learning, teaching, and achievement must be replaced with more modern, relevant policies, practices, and philosophies that are consistent with new views of intelligence.

Changing mental models requires both time and courage. The question most frequently asked about such a change is, "How will we find the time to do this work?" Because there is little hope of inventing more hours in the day, we must shift our models for how we use time in schools.

Consider how educators usually reflect on student work. Although grades and test scores tell us something about a student's learning, studying student work provides more important details. When we take the time to study student work in depth, we hear the student's voice, see the product of our intentions, and more fully feel the impact of our curriculum choices. Through studying student work one piece at a time, we learn a considerable amount about curriculum, instruction, and assessment. Many schools provide staff development time for this activity; many others do not.

Curriculum Redesign

Senge (1990) emphasizes that true learning organizations challenge existing mental models. The organization's leader, in an atmosphere of trust, challenges existing practices, assumptions, policies, and traditional ways of delivering the curriculum. Intellectual growth is found in "disequilibrium," not balance. Order is built out of chaos. Learning takes place, new understandings are forged, and new connections are bridged so that organizations function more consistently with their mission, vision, and goals. During these times of uncertainty, the habits of mind are most useful to and evident in a group's work.

In a school that is becoming a home for the mind, the core of the curriculum shifts from knowledge acquisition as an end to processes related to thinking: learning to learn, producing knowledge, transferring knowledge, making decisions, creating, problem solving as a group, and knowing how to behave when answers are not readily apparent. In the home for the mind, these processes are the subject matter of instruction. Content is selected because of its contributions to the habits of mind. Content becomes the vehicle to carry intellectual thought. The focus is on learning from the objectives instead of simply learning the objectives themselves.

These process-oriented goals cannot be assessed using product-oriented techniques. Thus, the existing evaluation paradigm must shift as well. In the home for the mind, assessment of students' growth focuses on students' learning becoming more conscious, more reflective, more efficient, more flexible, and more transferable (Costa & Kallick, 1995; Costa & Liebmann, 1997).

Teachers naturally assess achievement at the same level as their outcomes. Content-level measures, for example, assess the achievement of skills and knowledge. Process assessments require performance. Monitoring and assessing students' development of dispositions will require schools to systematically accumulate data over time, from multiple perspectives, and using a variety of techniques (such as portfolios, interviews, exhibitions, journal entries, and direct observation). School teams composed of administrators, support personnel, parents, and teachers from different grade levels and disciplines should design and report assessments for growth in the habits of mind.

SCHOOL CULTURE

Celebrate what you want to see more of.

Tom Peters

Infusing the habits of mind into the school and community involves a special effort to "re-culture" the school. Hidden, but powerful, cues in the school environment signal the institution's true culture. Efforts to enhance the staff's instructional competencies, develop the curriculum, revise instructional materials, and change assessment procedures are important components in the process of educational reengineering. But first, the school culture must be aligned with the habits of mind.

For example, personnel practices should reflect a desire to infuse the habits of mind. Job specifications for new personnel should include skills in teaching thinking. Administrators should encourage an atmosphere that honors all staff members' roles as professional decision-makers. Texts, tests, instructional materials, and other media should be selected with an eye toward their contributions to enhancing the habits of mind. Counseling, discipline, media, and psychological services all should be evaluated for their enhancement of and consistency with the habits.

Adopt discipline practices that encourage students to manage their impulsivity and empathize with others. Students can help generate rational, compassionate classroom and school rules. They can also be involved in evaluating their own behavior in relation to those criteria.

The habits of mind are valuable for classified staff members as well. A principal of one "thinking school" reported that a newly hired custodian constantly asked her to check on how well he was cleaning the classrooms and to tell him whether he was doing an adequate job. She decided to help him develop a clear mental image of what a clean classroom would look like. Then she worked to enhance his ability to evaluate for himself how well the room he cleaned fit that image.

Core values are communicated by what is appreciated and celebrated. Ritual and humor are important elements of the school culture. The value of the habits of mind is exemplified in a variety of traditions, celebrations, and humorous events that indicate thoughtful behavior is being achieved. Teachers and administrators can share personal, humorous anecdotes of their own lack of thinking. At school assemblies, faculty can honor students, teachers, and other staff members for acts of creativity, cooperation, thoughtfulness, innovation, and scholarly accomplishments. Academic decathlons, thinking fairs, problem-solving tournaments, debates, invention conventions, science fairs, art exhibitions, and musical programs all can celebrate the benefits of the habits of mind.

COMMUNICATION AND COLLABORATION

Professional collaboration at the district level is evident when teachers and administrators from different schools, subject areas, and grade levels meet to work with the habits of mind across all content areas and in all district policies and practices. Committees and advisory groups can assess staff needs, identify and locate talent, and participate in district-level decisions and prioritizing. These groups can also support school-site efforts; plan districtwide inservice sessions; and develop an aligned, coordinated, and developmentally appropriate curriculum for students.

COLLABORATION AND STAFF

Fostering collaboration among staff members is vital. All members of the school community must be committed to improving school climate, interpersonal relationships, and the quality of human interaction. Both students and staff will foster collaboration by working on the habit of thinking and communicating with clarity and precision. They can further collaboration by practicing and improving their listening skills of paraphrasing, empathizing, and clarifying.

Each group member's opinion must be respected. Create an atmosphere where disagreements can be stated without fear of damaging the relationship. Encourage debates and alternate points of view. Demonstrate how responsibility for errors, omissions, and inadequacies can be owned without blaming others. Model responses so that staff members learn that new ideas can be advanced without fear of criticism or judgment. Make group members' differing priorities, values, logic, and philosophical beliefs the topics of analysis, dialogue, understanding, and further questions.

Review and recommend instructional materials that will support development of the habits of mind. Encourage teachers to share information and materials through districtwide networks. At the school site, guide teachers to plan, prepare, and evaluate teaching materials. Enable them to visit each other's classrooms frequently to observe the relationship between instructional decision making and student behaviors. Encourage colleagues to prepare, develop, remodel, and rehearse lessons and units of study together.

Teachers and administrators should continue to discuss and refine their visions about thinking and evaluating that thinking. Child study teams can keep portfolios of students' work and discuss students' developmental thought processes and learning styles. They can also explore instructional problems and generate experimental solutions. Hold faculty meetings in classrooms where the host teacher shares instructional practices, materials, and videotaped lessons. Encourage teachers to sequence, articulate, prioritize, and plan for continuity and reinforcement of the habits of mind across grade levels and subject areas.

COLLABORATION AND THE COMMUNITY

Because parents are a child's first teacher, they probably most affect a child's inclination toward certain patterns of intellectual behavior. By the time children enter school, their cognitive structures, dispositions, and values may have been well formed. Educating parents about their dominant role as mediators of their children's cognitive development must be a significant part of the school-home connection.

Teachers and administrators should help parents understand that basic skills are the vehicles by which the school is teaching more enduring, lifelong, essential skills. Parents soon realize that the habits of mind are basic for survival in their children's chaotic, complex, and uncertain future. Habits of mind are required for success in college or a career. The habits are prerequisite to mastery in all school subjects, and career security and advancement depend on habits such as persisting, thinking and communicating with clarity and precision, thinking interdependently, and remaining open to continuous learning.

COMMUNICATION ABOUT GROWTH

In the school that is a home for the mind, the habits of mind pervade all forms of communication. Report cards, parent conferences, and other progress reports include indicators of students' growth in the habits of mind.

Teachers can collect portfolios of students' work over time as sources of data about the habits of mind. Schools can hold parent education meetings to show parents how to enhance their child's intelligent behavior. Use every means of communication possible: newspaper articles, school calendars, and classroom newsletters. Each type of communication should emphasize the school's vision—and progress—related to the habits of mind. Ask students to keep journals to record their own thinking and metacognition and to share and compare their growth of insight, creativity, and problem-solving strategies. Invite parents, too, to collect evidence of how their children's intellectual growth has been transferred from family to home situations.

LEADERSHIP

Because school leaders strongly influence curriculum and instruction, they also strongly influence students' learning, even though they don't teach in a classroom every day. Administrators constantly signal a value system to staff, students, and community, and they serve as significant role models for others to emulate. Leaders can deliberately influence critical decisions and practices related to the habits of mind in four ways: managing, monitoring, mediating, and modeling.

MANAGING

Leaders in the school that is a home for the mind make deliberate decisions about managing resources to broaden, heighten, and enhance the habits of mind. These leaders are alert for every opportunity to broaden group or individual outcomes.

Sometimes leaders specifically articulate beliefs about a school's enduring outcomes and essential learnings. Such efforts may appear in documents that drive conversations, decisions, assessments, and reporting in all curriculum and instructional practices. The leader can activate study groups to help staff members stay current with emerging literature and to contrast and align current practice with more recent findings. At other times, leaders offer direct instruction about the habits of mind. For example, they might teach about the habits in staff development programs, orientations for new faculty members, PTO meetings, or with any curriculum group.

Some leaders deliberately structure work so that stakeholders from diverse levels of maturity, beliefs, and styles must collaborate. Teachers from different disciplines and grade levels might be paired in peer coaching and other collaborative arrangements, which encourages using the habits of mind.

Leaders can also structure the environment to maximize certain forms of interactions. For example, situating classrooms around a common teacher workroom enhances interdependent thinking. A single lab shared by all science teachers and students increases the opportunity to draw from one content area and apply learnings to a variety of other content areas. Schools can be designed to build flexibility into the very walls and passages of the building, making it necessary for the staff, students, and community to function in cooperative ways (Saban, 1997).

MONITORING

Successful leaders constantly monitor themselves, their interactions with others, the allocation of available resources, and the environment for indicators of the level of outcomes being described, cited, reinforced, or valued. Self-monitoring implies asking yourself, "What are my intentions and motives at this moment?" Self-monitoring means keeping the habits of mind ever-ready as a template for decision making and problem solving.

Self-monitoring also implies being aware of your own words, values, and actions. "Monitoring metaphors" implies listening to others' words (and thus their implicit thoughts) for indicators that the habits of mind are being incorporated into a wide range of decisions and choices. For example, a leader should be alert to a teacher's language when describing a plan for instruction. Probing into the lesson's purposes and assessment strategies may disclose the level of thought at which the lesson is directed. Figure 2.1 contains examples of words and assessments to listen and look for in your search for the habits of mind.

Monitoring the allocation of resources means being alert to where money and time are invested. By comparing the stated outcomes and intentions of published materials, computer programs, curriculum guides, and descriptions of staff development opportunities with the habits of mind, leaders can select resources that will contribute to and further goals related to the habits.

MEDIATING

People who want to improve their craft never lose sight of the need for mediating, coaching, or mentoring. Athletes, musicians, and dancers all profit from coaching. Teachers profit from coaching, too.

FIGURE 2.1
Metaphors Showing the Habits of Mind

Level of Thought	Listen for These Words About Objectives	Look for These Types of Assessment
Activities	Pay attention, participate, complete, stay on task, take notes.	Teacher observation, counting, recording.
Content	Know about, understand, comprehend, grasp, remember.	Quizzes, tests of knowledge.
Process	Infer, conclude, criticize, explain, interpret, hypothesize, reason, analyze, support with evidence.	Performances, applications, exhibitions.
Habits of Mind	Develop perseverance, manage impulsivity, reflect, become more intellectually strategic.	Demonstrations over time, anecdotal records, rubrics, portfolios, checklists, self-assessments, metacognitive maps.

Source: Adapted from Costa & Garmston, 1998, p. 16.

Effective teachers working in isolation cannot create cohesive instructional patterns. Evered and Selman (1989) note, "The current management culture, with its focus on controlling behavior, needs to be replaced by a management culture in which skillful coaching creates the climate, environment, and context that empowers employees and teams to generate results."

Unfortunately, classrooms are often lonely places where other adults seldom witness a teacher's most creative work. Coaching "deprivatizes" the teaching act (Garmston & Wellman, 1999). Mediating is an intervention in which the dialogue centers on the enhancement of teaching, learning, and curriculum (Costa & Garmston, 1994). To mediate is to interpose oneself between a set of learners and the environment and, through nonjudgmental questioning, paraphrasing, and clarifying, draw attention to data that engage and transform thinking and meaning (Feuerstein, Feuerstein, & Schur, 1997). From such transformed meaning comes a reexamination of practices and their congruence with values. Figure 2.2 (see p. 22) shows how a leader's questions can be designed to engage higher levels of thinking.

MODELING

Leaders must walk their talk. Probably the most powerful intervention is for leaders to behave in a manner consistent with their beliefs and values. Whether leaders realize it or not, staff members, students, and community members are constantly alert to cues that signal congruence between the habits of mind and the leader's overt behaviors.

When problems arise in the school, community, and classroom, leaders must be observed solving those problems in intelligent ways. If not, the leaders themselves may unknowingly undermine the goals they're working so hard to promote. Thus, leaders must emulate all the habits of mind they hope to find in students and teachers.

Leaders can demonstrate their continuous learning by publicly stating their outcomes in the broadest terms and explaining the reasoning behind their actions. They can specify the habits of mind they are working with and make public the rationale for choosing them, asking others to provide feedback about their efforts (Hayes, 1995).

The habit of managing impulsivity is important to school leaders. Being a school principal is like living in a popcorn popper. So much is happening so quickly in so many different areas, leaders easily become tense, fatigued, and cognitively overloaded. Effective leaders develop self-awareness and biofeedback strategies to manage their impulsivity, remain poised, and cope with irritating problems.

FIGURE 2.2
Mediating Through Questions

When You Hear the Lesson Is . . .	And You Want to Raise It to . . .	Mediate by Asking Such Questions as . . .
Activity	Content	How will students benefit from engaging in this activity?
		What concepts do you want students to learn as a result of these activities?
Content	Processes	How will students demonstrate their understanding of these concepts?
		How will students apply these concepts in future lessons?
		What cognitive processes will students use to understand these concepts?
Processes	Habits of mind	What habits do you want students to form as a result of engaging in these processes?
		What enduring learnings will students gain by engaging in these processes?
		What do you want students to carry forth to future life situations?
		What personal values and habits will students form as a result of this lesson?
		How will this help your students become better human beings?

Source: Adapted from Costa & Garmston, 1998, p. 16.

Behaving empathically requires overcoming one's own egocentrism, detecting another person's subtle emotional and physical cues, and perceiving a situation from another's point of view. When dealing with parents, staff, colleagues, and students, the administrator who demonstrates empathy models one of the most important habits of mind. Administrators demonstrate metacognition when they publicly share their own planning strategies; when they admit their lack of knowledge and describe means of generating that knowledge; and when they engage others in deliberating, monitoring, and evaluating problem-solving strategies.

It was once thought that leadership was invested in a few individuals at the top of the organizational hierarchy and that the position of leadership was earned by position, credentials, or the number of academic degrees. In a school that is a home for the mind, however, all community members play all the roles. Leadership is a shared function: in meetings, staff development activities, action research, networking, and classrooms (Garmston & Wellman, 1999; Lambert, 1998). Intellectual shifts result when schools redefine the identities and roles of the participants in the educational process: students, teachers, administrators, and trustees. All these members of the school community can take on the following leadership roles:

• *Facilitating.* Conducting meetings for the purpose of shared decision making, planning, or problem solving.

• *Presenting.* Teaching groups to develop knowledge, skills, or attitudes that they can apply in their work.

• *Coaching.* Helping valued colleagues travel from where they are to where they want to be. Serving as a coach means mediating—not judging—a colleague's decisions, intellectual functions, and perceptions (Costa & Garmston, 1994).

• *Consulting.* Sharing expertise in a relationship and acting as one of the following: an information specialist who delivers technical knowledge, an advocate for content who will influence the group using broad knowledge, or an advocate for process.

• *Networking.* Paying attention to the flow and interchange of energy. Knowing about colleagues' talents, information, and resources allows the networker to link people and groups together in mutually supportive relationships.

• *Researching.* Helping individuals and groups make meaning by generating, interpreting, validating, and owning data. Researching creates a situation in which people learn with a higher degree of rigor because they must make meaning.

RESOURCEFUL SCHOOL COMMUNITY

How school personnel expend their most valuable resources signals to staff members, the community, and students what is truly valued. In many schools, the most valuable resources are energy, money, and time—and time is the most precious of the three. Liberating these elusive resources from within the school community usually requires administrators and teachers to exercise many habits of mind: creating, imagining, innovating; thinking flexibly; questioning and posing problems; and persisting.

ENERGY

Involving parents and the community in building and "owning" the school's vision liberates their power, talent, and energy. When parents understand that the habits of mind are important outcomes for themselves *and* their children, they willingly devote their energies to supporting their child's learning at home and at school. Schools can tap into the community's energy in a variety of ways:

• Invite local realtors to bring new families to visit the school so they can become acquainted with the school's mission, goals, and outcomes— and how they can participate in this important work, too.
• Establish partnerships with local businesses, organizations, and universities to support the habits of mind.
• Ask parents to catalog community resources that could support learning about the habits of mind (including possible field trips, local experts, and interested service clubs).
• Seek volunteers who are anxious to share their talents for the school's "good cause" in all areas of the community, not just among parents.
• Invite parents into the classrooms to read books and stories that illuminate the virtues of the habits of mind.

MONEY

Most extra financing for schools comes in the form of grants from philanthropic, state, and national sources. Schools find it more challenging to mobilize local resources. Bake sales and car washes are traditional ways of raising money. Yet we've seen creative, imaginative staff and community members seek many other different sources of funding:

• One school asked real estate agents to notify them when houses were

24

sold so that they could seek donations from the proceeds of the home-owners' moving day sales.

• Some parents sell advertising space in the PTO newsletter to local businesses.

• In one community, the school worked with automobile dealers so that $50 was donated to the school each time parents purchased a car locally.

• Working with a local book store, a school reserved a night for teachers to use $250 raised by the PTO to browse and purchase books for the school at a discount.

• In another district, parents found the financial resources to hire substitutes so that teachers could be released to visit and coach each other. Staff members and parents were also sent to workshops, courses, conferences, and other inservice opportunities to learn more about developing intellectual skills and the habits of mind.

TIME

You will never "find" time for anything. If you want the time, you must make it.

Charles Buxton

When school staff members are truly committed to developing the habits of mind as a shared vision, they devote their precious time to understanding, supporting, and assessing the habits. We've seen staff members generate many innovative ways of organizing time:

• One school lengthened some days so that the school day could be shortened one day a week for staff development and enrichment.

• Another school invited parents and resource personnel to teach classes, which freed teachers for meeting, planning, and coaching each other.

• Some teachers specifically budget time to meet together throughout the week. Three days a week are used for curriculum planning, one day a week is used for discussion about students, and one day a week is used for studying student work.

• In some schools, social and working meetings are combined into weekend retreats and evening events so that agendas are accomplished in a pleasant atmosphere.

Too often, faculty meeting time is relegated to managerial tasks and transmission of information. Encouraging teachers to discuss the habits of mind as a total faculty or in departments or grade-level meetings is time well spent. For example, here's what you might do:

• Ask teachers to report what they learned in courses, staff development activities, or through reading.

• Invite teachers to describe successes and problems in attempting to teach for habits of mind.

• Decide the habits of mind on which to focus this year.

• Demonstrate instructional techniques that provoke discussions of the habits of mind.

• Compare how teachers include the habits of mind in each subject area.

• Describe how students increase in complexity of intellectual skills throughout their development.

• Review and select materials to enhance the habits of mind.

• Discuss ways to support each other's teaching with concurrent instruction (thinking across the curriculum).

CONTINUOUS LEARNING

The solution is to empower teachers, to help them develop an internalized locus of control. Teachers and principals, supervisors and superintendents, boards of education and state legislators all must appreciate the possibilities of school improvement efforts that marshal the motivations and unleash the talents of those who work directly with children day after day.

Frymier, 1987

Continuous learning implies an atmosphere of trust, risk taking, and inquiry. In this sort of atmosphere, data are generated without fear that they will be used to evaluate success or failure. Creativity is also more likely to grow in this type of low-risk environment. For too long, though, continuous learning has been hindered by a move to quantify and rank school effectiveness.

Student achievement and teachers' competence often are determined by a narrow range of standardized test scores in a limited number of content areas: reading, math, and language acquisition. This assessment process is external to teachers' goal setting, curriculum, and instructional decision making. Even more pressure is applied when achievement test results are published in newspapers, and awards of excellence are granted to schools showing the highest gains in test scores.

Teachers have become disenfranchised through this process. They have little to say about what these tests measure, and test content usually is irrelevant to their curriculum. The results of such tests disclose little about the adequacy of a teacher's instructional decisions. In effect, the tests tell teachers they are "incompetent" to assess student achievement on their own, and the observations they make in the classroom every day are suspect and inconsequential.

The accountability movement sent educators searching for "hard data" by which to assess their efforts. What teachers observed came to be considered "soft data." Yet we believe the "hardest," most valuable data available may be the information collected by an *enlightened* teaching team that systematically gathers results over time in the real-life, day-to-day interactions and problem solving of the classroom.

To encourage continuous learning for students and staff, teachers must be allowed to design strategies for collecting data. Then they must be allowed to use that assessment data to guide their informed, reflective practice. Encourage staff members to design feedback spirals that (1) include multiple ways of gathering data and (2) establish criteria for judgment.

Staff members can work together to develop a common understanding, reliability of observations, and reporting of results. Encourage teachers to be researchers. Teachers become researchers when they test alternate classroom arrangements and instructional strategies. Their colleagues share in this research when they observe the experimentation and talk about the results. Staff members can experiment with various lesson designs, instructional sequences, and teaching materials to determine their effects on small groups of students. Or, they can collaborate with colleagues to conduct experiments with large-group instruction.

Human beings are made to be different. Diversity is the basis of biological survival. Each of us has a different genetic structure; unique facial features; a distinguishing thumb print; a distinctive signature; diverse backgrounds of knowledge, experience, and culture; and a preferred way of gathering, processing, and expressing information and knowledge. We even have a singular frequency in which we vibrate (Leonard, 1978). Leaders are sensitive to and capitalize on these differences to enhance intellectual growth.

Organizational life might seem easier if all members of the learning community thought and acted in a similar fashion and if they remained in their own departments and grade levels. Time limitations, the isolation of classrooms, and our obsession with the archaic compartmentalization of disciplines and grades keep school staffs separated. Thus, opportunities for teachers' intellectual growth are limited. Schools that are home for the mind break down these barriers.

In schools that are home for the mind, the habits of mind develop through resolving differences, achieving consensus, and stretching to accommodate dissonance. Staff members come to realize greater growth is possible when they bridge their differences. (Some businesses engage in what is referred to as "skunkworks," deliberately bringing together personnel from different departments, positions, and levels to make connections and find new and divergent ways to solve problems.)

Interdependent learning communities are built by valuing the friction that differences bring and by resolving those differences in an atmosphere of trust and reciprocity. A school becomes a home for the mind only when the total community is an intellectually stimulating environment for all the participants. A school becomes a home for the mind when every community member realizes that liberating human intellectual potential is the goal of education—and when they use their energies to enhance the habits of mind of themselves *and* others.

REFERENCES

Cawelti, G. (1995). *Handbook of research on improving student achievement.* Arlington, VA: Educational Research Service.

Costa, A., & Garmston, R. (1994). *Cognitive coaching: A foundation for Renaissance schools.* Norwood, MA: Christopher Gordon Publishers.

Costa, A., & Garmston, R. (1998, Spring). Maturing outcomes. *Encounter: Education for Meaning and Social Justice 11*(1), 10–18.

Costa, A., & Kallick, B. (1995). *Assessment in the learning organization: Shifting the paradigm.* Alexandria, VA: Association for Supervision and Curriculum Development.

Costa, A., & Liebmann, R. (Eds.). (1997). *Envisioning process as content: Toward a Renaissance curriculum.* Thousand Oaks, CA: Corwin Press.

Evered, R., & Selman, J. (1989, Autumn). Coaching and the art of management. *Organizational Dynamics 18*, 16–32.

Feuerstein, R., Feuerstein, R., & Schur, Y. (1997). Process as content in education, particularly for retarded performers. In A. Costa & R. Liebmann (Eds.), *Supporting the spirit of learning: When process is content* (pp. 1–22). Thousand Oaks, CA: Corwin Press.

Frymier, J. (1987, September). Bureaucracy and the neutering of teachers. *Phi Delta Kappan, 69*(1), 10.

Fullan, M. (1993). *Change forces.* New York: Falmer Press.

Garmston, R., & Wellman, B. (1999). *Adaptive schools.* Norwood, MA: Christopher Gordon Publishers.

Hayes, C. (1995, Spring). Public coaching as a tool for organization development. *Journal of Staff Development 16*(2), 44–49.

Lambert, L. (1998). *Building leadership capacity in schools.* Alexandria, VA: Association for Supervision and Curriculum Development.

Leonard, G. (1978). *The silent pulse: A search for the perfect rhythm that exists in each of us.* New York: Bantam Books.

Louis, K. S., Marks, H. M., & Kruse, S. (1996). Teacher's professional community in restructuring schools. *American Educational Research Journal 33*(4), 757–798.

Saban, J. (1997). Process pervades the organization: Capturing the spirit. In A. Costa & R. Liebmann (Eds.), *The process centered school: Sustaining a Renaissance community* (pp. 172–188). Thousand Oaks, CA: Corwin Press.

Saphier, J., & King, M. (1985, March). Good seeds grow in strong cultures. *Educational Leadership (42)*6, 67–74.

Senge, P. (1990). *The fifth discipline.* New York: Doubleday.

3

BRINGING TO LIFE A VISION

CURTIS SCHNORR AND THOMMIE DEPINTO PIERCY

S everal years ago, Friendship Valley Elementary School in Westminster,
Maryland, was just a partially completed shell. The new building
obviously lacked a physical core at this point, but the school lacked a
spiritual core, too. The building had been assigned a principal but no staff
members or students. As construction crews shaped the outward appear-
ance of Friendship Valley, the principal, and eventually the staff, needed to
create a vision for why Friendship Valley had been built and what the
school would achieve once students walked through its doors.

Senge (1990) says that in its simplest form, a vision answers the question, "What do we want to create?" (p. 206). He believes a vision generates
a sense of commonality that permeates the organization. Wheatley (1992)
describes a vision as organizational clarity about purpose and direction.
Where would Friendship Valley finds its clarity, purpose, and direction?

The search ended soon after a presentation by Arthur Costa on
"Creating Schools as Homes for the Mind." Staff members read *The School
as a Home for the Mind* (Costa, 1991) several times, and they identified key
features of a home for the mind. As construction crews finished building
the physical shell of Friendship Valley, staff members enthusiastically took
up the work of constructing a home for the mind inside the new school's
classrooms, offices, and halls.

REFINING THE VISION

The precepts of a home for the mind are simply stated, but they hold a
powerful message. Many of Friendship Valley's new staff members found
they shared in these beliefs. These professionals had reached a crossroads in
their careers, and they wanted a new direction for their work. The vision of
a home for the mind sparked a deep sense of purposefulness for them, and

they drew tremendous energy from that vision.

Staff members were encouraged to examine what they had done in their professional lives to this point and how they might do their work differently. All teachers received copies of *The School as a Home for the Mind* (Costa, 1991), which included the chapter "The Search for Intelligent Life" (pp. 19–31). Costa's work provided a framework for inquiry and dialogue as staff members considered two important questions: (1) What do you really want Friendship Valley to be? and (2) What will students and staff look like in this school?

As staff members answered these questions, their focus kept returning to the habits of mind (which are described as "intelligent behaviors" in *The School as a Home for the Mind*). The habits supported all these professionals believed in, and they saw that the habits clearly would benefit staff members *and* students. Thus, the habits of mind became a vital building block in Friendship Valley's home for the mind. The habits of mind created a common language of enthusiasm, hope, and commitment. Staff members soon believed the habits were a wonderful vehicle for taking the school's vision off the wall and into the classrooms and community of Friendship Valley.

TRANSFORMING THE VISION INTO CULTURE AND PRACTICE

From the beginning of their work, Friendship Valley's administrators promoted a culture that fostered trust and intellectual curiosity, embraced conflict and diversity, encouraged collaboration and cooperation, and reveled in caring and celebrating. This culture could not have been developed without the habits of mind. The habits were institutionalized into the school's culture and practice through four avenues: distributed leadership, open and honest dialogue, cognitive coaching, and staff development.

DISTRIBUTED LEADERSHIP

Creating a safe learning environment and helping others succeed are key elements of a leader's role. Administrators established several important norms that encouraged faculty members to take increased decision-making responsibility. Each norm reinforced one or more of the habits of mind. As a result of following the norms, committees and teams became more dynamic and successful, and staff members took the initiative for problem solving. Here are the norms:

• Membership on the School Improvement Team (SIT), which is the central nervous system of the school, was open to all staff members. Because everyone had the opportunity to be included in policy-level decision making, all staff members felt empowered. This norm encouraged the habits of thinking flexibly; listening with understanding and empathy; and creating, imagining, innovating.

• Grade-level, team facilitator positions were open to all faculty members. This decision called upon the habits of thinking flexibly, taking responsible risks, and thinking interdependently.

• Schedules and schoolwide policies were open to suggestions for change. Administrators drew on the habits of applying past knowledge to new situations and questioning and posing problems.

• Teachers created the school handbook, and staff members—not administrators—drafted school policies. Carrying out this norm required the habits of listening with understanding and empathy, questioning and posing problems, remaining open to continuous learning, and taking responsible risks.

OPEN AND HONEST DIALOGUE

"Roundtable dialogues" furthered the development of trust among staff members. These voluntary roundtables focused on relevant topics and provided a context for lively discussion. The roundtables also supported staff development and offered an opportunity to practice open, honest dialogue. Professional use of several habits of mind evolved through these roundtables: persisting, questioning and posing problems, listening with understanding and empathy, and managing impulsivity.

The roundtables began when a faculty member suggested that staff members discuss a relevant topic and a related article, such as Costa and Garmston's (1998) "Maturing Outcomes." The article was distributed for staff members to read before the roundtable. As they prepared for the meeting, participants privately chose one habit of mind to focus on during the discussion.

To start a roundtable meeting, the facilitator posed an open-ended question to spark the group's discussion. Staff members were encouraged to openly and honestly share insights, humor, support, or reservations about the topic at hand. Teachers often remained in the media center after the roundtable to continue their dialogue with colleagues rather than linger in the parking lot. Participants left the roundtables with much more than knowledge about a topic. They gained trust in their colleagues, and they fostered collegiality with other staff members.

COGNITIVE COACHING

To teach students the habits of mind, teachers themselves must practice in an intellectually stimulating environment. Cognitive coaching fostered this kind of environment, and this approach became a cornerstone for enhancing teachers' intellectual capacities.

As part of the coaching process, each teacher scheduled a planning conference with an administrator. Then the teacher completed a planning conference sheet that included provocative questions to spark ideas. The planning conference was held before a classroom observation. Classroom observation provided the opportunity for collecting data about the teaching behaviors and the student learning discussed in the planning conference. A reflecting conference was held after the observation to allow teachers the opportunity to share impressions of the lesson, data, and future planning.

Teachers monitored their own behaviors and progress toward their goals. As they proceeded from the planning stage to implementing their lessons to reflecting on their learning, they found that the processes of cognitive coaching reinforced the habits of mind. For example, as one teacher coached another, the teacher might focus on listening with understanding and empathy. Or, the teacher might guide the person being coached to think flexibly about the lesson being planned. When another coach shared data, that person might use the habit of thinking and communicating with clarity and precision. Finally, the entire coaching conference could be a model for practicing the habit of remaining open to continuous learning.

STAFF DEVELOPMENT

At Friendship Valley, teachers are viewed as leaders committed to achieving the school's vision inside their classrooms. Teachers were encouraged to accept greater responsibility for student achievement. They truly were invested in this effort because they helped determine school improvement outcomes, identified strategies to drive the outcomes, exercised professional judgment about curriculum content, and were responsible for instructional decisions. Administrators furthered this atmosphere in five specific ways:

• Encouraged collaboration among grade levels by establishing common staff development strategies and resources.
• Supported teacher experimentation and autonomy; they defined "failures" as opportunities to learn.
• Modeled and supported professional behaviors related to caring, optimism, humor, and friendliness.
• Minimized the threat of risk taking.

• Encouraged solving school problems through effective communication and group decision making.

Eventually, all staff development initiatives were selected with an eye toward how they could further the school's work with the habits of mind. This staff development occurred in stages. For example, administrators first provided staff members with a foundation in the habits of mind through articles, texts, and videos. The habits were reinforced with large wall charts, small desktop models, and samples of instruction that integrated the habits of mind.

Risk taking was supported with the help of Toni Worsham, director of the Maryland Center for Thinking Studies at Coppin State College in Baltimore, Maryland. Her site visits were followed with informal, after-school sessions where she and faculty members discussed instructional decision-making and delivery techniques. Having a professional consultant support the vision through workshops, classroom visits, and a graduate course provided the momentum to continue risk taking.

The next stage of staff development provided direction in using visual tools for thinking. Staff members initially used Frank Lyman's (McTighe & Lyman, 1991) question/response cueing strategy. Lyman's question/response cues are graphic representations of seven different types of thought. These cues enable teachers to provide instruction on different types of thought, and the cues offer students a vehicle to comprehend texts at higher levels of thinking. Lyman's classroom visits supported teachers in their instructional decisions. After-school sessions allowed time to question and ponder future instructional directions.

David Hyerle introduced the staff to Thinking Maps®, visual tools that collect and organize thought into visual patterns (Hyerle, 1995). Students used the maps to construct, discuss, and assess their thinking. Such work created a subtle shift in communication, which could be seen everywhere: in students' thinking displayed in the hallways, during small-group literature discussions, and during the faculty's school improvement meetings.

Professional development included numerous full-day visits by a variety of presenters who stayed for after-school faculty gatherings to explore topics in depth. This on-site professional development proved so successful that it evolved into a staff development norm for the school.

Each type of staff development contributed to specific learnings by the faculty. The combined staff development deepened understanding of the habits of mind. Ultimately, developing professional capacities with the habits of mind resulted in students using the habits of mind. Student use in turn resulted in improved student achievement and community involvement.

INFLUENCING STUDENTS AND COMMUNITY

Schools need community support. From the moment Friendship Valley opened, staff members worked to share their energy and excitement about the new school and its unique approach. Even before the building opened, a teacher created a videotape depicting the distinctive elements of Friendship Valley, and showing how the school would serve students and the community. This video was shown to students and community groups months before the school opened. The presentation usually was their first encounter with the precepts of a home for the mind and the habits of mind.

Staff members believed everyone in the school community had to understand these precepts. Teachers and administrators used newsletters, parent information nights, and student displays to further their message about the habits of mind. In time, students became the most powerful messengers about the habits. Parents saw that their children were excited about learning each and every day. From the very first day, staff members at Friendship Valley worked to create what Perkins (1992) calls "a climate that fosters an energetic culture of thoughtful teaching and learning" (p. 112). This climate sparked students' enthusiasm about the power of thinking and learning.

Staff members used every opportunity to emphasize their commitment to the habits of mind. Before the first open house, they hung posters about the habits of mind throughout the hallways. On the first day of school, students took home messages about the habits of mind. Staff members wrote newspaper articles about the habits. Office referrals underscored the habits of mind. Students weren't simply disciplined; they were asked to problem solve using habits of mind that would serve them better if a similar situation arose again. The school's message was clear, consistent, and simple: The habits of mind can be used in every facet of staff members' and students' daily lives, both in and out of school.

LOOKING FOR RESULTS

Although the staff and administration were determined to stay the course with the habits of mind, they understood that they had to show results, too. At first, results were seen in ways that couldn't be quantified. Students began to question more intelligently through using precise language. They treated others with empathy and respect, as evidenced by their decreased impulsivity and how they truly listened to what others had to say. Students began to enjoy problem solving, and they spent more time seeking solutions when an answer was not readily apparent. Creativity was on display throughout the classrooms and hallways in art projects, extended learning projects, physical activity, and song and music. Students talked about how they used the habits of mind at home, and they even described how their parents sometimes failed to use the habits!

Although these results were satisfying and important, staff members understood that the true judgment would come from the school's results on state-mandated tests. Results from the first year yielded scores that were above state and county averages in all areas. Performance on these tests improved yearly. Ultimate recognition came from the state of Maryland in the form of a performance award for significant academic progress.

Friendship Valley Elementary School has come a long way since those first days when it was nothing more than a physical shell. Tour the building now and you'll see a vibrant home for the mind supported by the habits of mind. In kindergarten, students manage their impulsivity and use clear and precise language as they describe the flight of butterflies. In 1st grade, students enjoy problem solving as they graph the letters of their name. A 2nd grade math lesson begins with the teacher referring students to the directions on the board; he also reminds the children to turn on their habits of mind related to listening.

Third graders use all their senses as they watch their egg-crate parachutes float from the roof of the building. Fourth graders use creativity and prior knowledge in the wax museum they've created. Fifth graders use persistence and flexibility in their thinking during a unit on the Negro Baseball League. No classroom or office is untouched by the habits of mind: art, music, gym, media center, reading, speech and language, special education, and guidance counselor.

In the late spring of each year, teachers and other staff members gather to reflect on the current school year and plan for the next year. They always ask themselves several key questions: What impact have we made on student instruction and the development of a thinking school? What will we continue to value and respect as educators and a school? What has worked and allowed our school to be successful? Every year, the habits of mind are identified as a key ingredient in student and school success. Staff members at Friendship Valley continue to experiment with, refine their skills in, and look for new avenues to use the habits of mind as they continually remodel, renew, and recharge their home for the mind.

REFERENCES

Costa, A. (1991). *The school as a home for the mind*. Palatine, IL: SkyLight Publishers.

Costa, A., & Garmston, R. (1998). *Maturing outcomes*. Unpublished article.

Hyerle, D. (1995). *Thinking Maps® tools for learning*. Cary, NC: Innovative Sciences, Inc.

McTighe, J., & Lyman, F., Jr. (1991). Cueing thinking in the classroom: The promise of theory-embedded tools. In A. Costa (Ed.), *Developing minds: A resource book for teaching thinking* (Rev. ed., Vol. 1, pp. 243–250). Alexandria, VA: Association for Supervision and Curriculum Development.

Perkins, D. (1992). *Smart schools*. New York: Free Press.

Senge, P. (1990). *The fifth discipline*. New York: Doubleday.

Wheatley, M. (1992). *Leadership and the new science: Learning about organizations from an orderly universe*. San Francisco, CA: Berrett-Koehler Publishers.

4

INFUSING THE
HABITS OF MIND
INTO A SCHOOL CULTURE

DEBORAH HANSEN

*Schools that support the continuous learning and development of students
also support the continuous development of their educators. Schools must
be places of learning for both students and educators. You can't have one
without the other. Building a culture of professional learning in schools is
a necessary condition for sustained learning and particularly critical if we
are to link professional development with reformed concepts of teaching,
learning, and schooling.*

Margaret Arbuckle, in Robbins, 1998

At DeLong Middle School in Eau Claire, Wisconsin, such concepts
were especially important when we sought to infuse critical thinking and the habits of mind into our school culture.

GETTING STARTED

As coordinator of staff development for our building, I focused on how to
translate critical thinking into practice in our school. The administrative
team began by sharing a strategic plan with staff members. We formally
adopted critical thinking as a building goal. We familiarized ourselves with
the issues and strategies related to incorporating critical thinking skills
across the curriculum. At the same time, we identified individuals in our
building who were interested in critical thinking, had a background in

critical thinking, or displayed strong leadership talents.

We next formed two teams to help us move forward. The first was an advisory team made up of our administration and three people from the district's critical thinking leadership team. The second group was our building implementation team, with two administrators and several staff volunteers. This team is comprised of six to eight members, depending on the number of volunteers each year. Staff members may serve on the team as many years as they want, or they may rotate their participation.

Initially, the teams' major task was to develop a plan specific to our school. Our focusing question was, "How can we infuse critical thinking into our school culture at DeLong?" This question sparked several discussions about our ultimate vision, long-term plans, and short-term strategies.

We first defined the *what* of our vision. What exactly did we mean by infusing critical thinking? What specifically was our content? What would critical thinking look like in the school? Our next step addressed *how* we would accomplish our goals. We included specific strategies, and we considered how we could create a system to periodically evaluate our progress and define our next course of action. My description of our work in the remainder of this chapter follows the self-assessment model described in Chapter 1: approach, implementation, and results.

APPROACH

The building team began by defining what we meant by infusing critical thinking into the school culture. We agreed that the behaviors related to thinking critically would permeate everyday activities. An observer would see evidence of critical thinking in all classrooms. Interactions between individuals and in small groups would show the strategies of critical thinking in action. These interactions could be formal or informal, adult to adult, student to student, or adult to student. The interactions could also occur between two or more individuals. Ultimately, we wanted the use of critical thinking strategies to be instinctive to everyone in the building.

Our next step was to define the content we wanted to focus on. When we explored this point, we discovered that committee members had attended a variety of workshops with many critical thinking experts: Arthur Costa, Bena Kallick, Marian Leibowitz, Robert Marzano, Sandra Parks, and Richard Paul. We sifted through these experts' various models of critical thinking. Finally, we agreed that to get the majority of staff members to adopt the initiative, we needed to start with specific content that could easily be translated to all of our building's environments.

With this criterion in mind, we chose to start with Costa's habits of mind. Our primary reason was that the habits are straightforward, logical, easily translated into action, and appropriate across the curriculum. The fact that the habits also apply to all age levels made our selection even more appealing. The habits of mind would do more than strengthen instruction. They could be observed, they could be labeled, they could be modeled, and they could enhance the effectiveness of adult interactions.

Because we wanted critical thinking to permeate our whole school culture, we needed to choose content that applied in all situations. The habits of mind fit that criterion. The team members all read the chapter "The Search for Intelligent Life" (Costa, 1991a, pp. 19–31). We made available *Developing Minds: A Resource Book for Teaching Thinking* (Costa, 1991b) and *The School as a Home for the Mind* (Costa, 1991a).

From our reading, we began to specifically define what our building would look like if we infused the habits of mind into our culture. We began with the heart of our school: the classrooms. Individually and collectively, we considered what a classroom would look and sound like if the habits were used. We also considered what the school would look and sound like if the habits were absent. We discussed this topic as a group until everyone had a similar mental picture of classrooms where students and teachers used the habits of mind.

We expanded this discussion to consider how the habits of mind would look in faculty meetings, team and department meetings, parent conferences, and extracurricular settings. We believed staff members had to model the habits before they could expect students to use them consistently. We also believed staff members had to be able to describe the behaviors that define acting intelligently. For example, when language arts teachers describe students' editing efforts as careful and precise, we know they are talking about the habit of striving for accuracy. We were more interested in staff members being able to describe student behaviors related to the habits of mind than we were in having them label those behaviors with particular names.

IMPLEMENTATION

Our next step was to develop an action plan to accomplish our goal. Our team wanted to provide staff members with a wide variety of options, so we aimed to offer a continuum of services. Our action plan included access to written materials, staff development options in and out of the building, individualized growth plans, and reinforcement through supervision. We supported and encouraged district efforts with curriculum writing teams, evaluation committees, and materials adoption meetings. We also used the district leadership team as a source of recommendations for written materials, districtwide staff development options, and out-of-district staff development opportunities.

First, we expanded the school's professional library. As we found written materials that supported our efforts, we circulated them among staff members. We began with "The Search for Intelligent Life" (Costa, 1991a). We added many books to our professional library, and we sent out periodic reviews so staff members knew what was available.

Next, we made out-of-building staff development options available to small teams of staff members, and we encouraged participation in district activities. Because our community houses a state university with an excellent reputation in the field of education, our staff members have easy access to courses and outreach workshops. We maintain a reasonable building budget that allows many teachers to attend workshops each year. We have four half-days built into the school calendar for professional growth.

Focusing In-House

As our work continued, most of our efforts focused on developing an in-school staff development program. As we designed our model, we considered adult learning theory, the target content, various techniques and strategies, and the uniqueness of our staff. We identified the many and varied training opportunities available, and we tried to complement rather than duplicate them.

During our planning, we placed a high priority on increasing staff awareness and interest in topics related to critical thinking. We used time during our monthly staff and leadership council meetings to tell staff members about our committee's work. We also used these meetings to model the habits of mind for the staff.

Among our ideas was recruiting a variety of staff members to serve as resource people. These staff members would talk to colleagues about their training, share their own experiences implementing the habits of mind, plan with colleagues trying to incorporate new strategies, and act as a model for other staff members. We invited these resource people to facilitate staff development activities within our building. Though many staff members could have filled these roles, most were reluctant to be experts "at home." As a result, we began by using facilitators from the district leadership team. Our own resource people initially played a low-key role.

At this point, we collected a variety of information from staff members themselves. We conducted a simple survey that included teachers and paraprofessional staff members. We collected information about the amount of background knowledge an individual had about critical thinking, what information the individual desired to receive in the future, the best times to provide staff development opportunities for the individual, and what that individual would like to take away from a staff development opportunity.

After we compiled this information, we shared it with the staff. We divided the content into topic categories, explained the concept of a resource person—eliminating the expectation to facilitate workshops from the description—and asked for volunteers to act as resource people in each category. Fortunately, we had at least three volunteers for each topic. Our next step was to look for training opportunities for those people. All training sessions were attended by more than one person so the resource people could work cooperatively to increase their own levels of proficiency.

Offering Miniworkshops

At this point, our committee developed a miniworkshop model to serve all staff members in the building. Individuals sign up to participate in these workshops; they are not assigned. We offer the workshops in multiple time slots through a combination of release time with a substitute, after-school time, and time already designated for staff development.

A maximum of 15 people may participate in a workshop. Our average is 12 attendees. The general workshop format is the same for all topics, and it includes three to four half-day sessions facilitated by a team of two or more district or school employees.

As the first session begins, participants assess the group's knowledge. Then the presenter introduces the topic, including what the theory base is, how the topic relates to the habits of mind, and how the topic fits into the overall district model of critical thinking. All the facilitators use critical thinking strategies to convey their information, so participants see strong modeling.

We allow time for participants to process what they have learned and ask questions. Guided practice is provided within the session, often in small groups of two to four participants. Discussion time helps people process the practice activity. Depending on the topic, the workshop can take two or three sessions. We then ask participants to use the new theory, strategy, or technique in their own work setting.

The next session begins with the participants discussing their experiences. The group troubleshoots rough spots and sets goals. Participants are encouraged to work with each other or one of the resource people in the building. During and after the workshops, we provide print materials that support the topic. With more complex concepts, participants may reconvene after a semester or year of implementation.

Results

This program was piloted in the spring of 1995. Our first offering was a general introduction to critical thinking. The workshop included introducing the habits of mind and showing how to create a thinking environment. We repeated this offering twice during the 1995–96 school year, and then offered an advanced session for staff members who had participated in the introductory offering. We typically offer four workshops a year, periodically checking with staff members to see how their needs are changing.

Once they had a broad base of information about critical thinking, staff members expressed an interest in getting additional detailed information and attending workshops that provided a more intense focus on a single topic. We now offer topical workshops focused on specific strategies or techniques, including Socratic questioning, concept attainment, reflective practice, graphic organizers, differentiating instruction, brain-based learning, technology as a learning tool, and assessment. During each workshop, the theory and modeling are connected to the habits of mind and other basic critical thinking skills taught in the introductory workshops.

The building committee meets once or twice yearly to review staff members' input about the success of past programs and interest in future programs. We review changes in the district direction, new state requirements, and training requests that do not fall under the critical thinking category. Finally, we consider informal sources of feedback, such as reports of student behavior, information from parents and students, discussions at team and department meetings, and observations during daily interactions. Using all these sources, the committee plans the next group of miniworkshops.

Overcoming Obstacles

When we began providing miniworkshops in this small-group format, several staff members were apprehensive about participating. The biggest concern was working with such a small group. Staff members commented that having a small group required too much participation by individual participants. The bottom line was no one wanted to be embarrassed in front of their peers, and no one wanted the experience to add stress or pressure to their already demanding work life. These emotions echoed the feelings of the resource people who provided workshop support.

Though we wanted staff members to be comfortable and to attend additional workshops, we firmly believed the workshops were effective precisely because of the extensive participation they demanded. Once people overcame their reluctance and attended a collegial workshop that encouraged questioning, probing, and disagreement in a respectful manner, they found the workshops stimulating. After the first couple of workshops, word-of-mouth endorsement by past participants encouraged others to sign up for future opportunities.

We were careful to provide resource people with the support and time they needed to prepare for sharing in a group. We structured sharing to focus on the successes and obstacles the resource people faced during implementation without making them responsible for sharing content. This structure removed some of the threat and anxiety the resource people felt. When they realized we wanted both their positive and negative experiences, they knew they were not expected to reflect a perfect model but rather a work in progress. Once they shared their experiences, a natural discussion flowed from the group. This discussion was a combination of support, questions, and "what ifs." The resource people have reported positive reactions to these discussions, and many have expanded their role to include facilitating workshops.

Because our structure allows a free give-and-take of information throughout the workshop, the facilitators have reported that this kind of exchange challenges their thinking and causes them to reach a deeper understanding of the concepts. Participants often identify the small, collegial groups as a key element in the success of the miniworkshops. The intimacy of the groups gives participants a natural support group for their future implementation efforts.

An added bonus has been our team structure and our special needs inclusion programs. Because core academic teachers and special needs teachers serve on interdisciplinary teams, two or more team members will often register together for a workshop. Their daily common planning time allows them to collaborate smoothly on implementing the concepts they learned in the training. The team structure they participate in daily allows them to share their new learning with other members of their team. This sharing often results in additional team members signing up for future workshops.

Increasing numbers of staff members have asked for miniworkshops. They suggest content for new sessions, request follow-up sessions, and request to have workshops repeated. Some of our requests come from return participants, but many are from first-time participants who are interested because of what they have seen or heard from their colleagues.

Though this interest in the miniworkshops continues to grow, we have not been able to offer more than four in a year. Our biggest obstacles are scheduling participants, resource teachers, and facilitators for multiple days of meetings. With the busy schedules of so many different individuals, it is difficult to avoid conflicts when choosing dates. Another obstacle to finding dates is the district's substitute teacher shortage. To acquire enough strong substitutes, we must avoid all the meeting dates for other buildings, sports tournaments, and major conventions. Though the logistics of scheduling are frequently trying, the benefits of these workshops far outweigh the frustrations of coordinating them.

WALKING THE TALK

Our administrative team has made an effort to be visible and participate in miniworkshop discussions whenever possible. In addition, we have used our role in supervision to encourage participants about their experiences in the workshops and their implementation efforts. We have offered support by facilitating time for individuals to meet with other participants. We encourage individuals to use staff development time to plan for implementation, and we recognize and reinforce efforts we observe in the classroom. We have volunteered support in a variety of other ways:

• Observe in classrooms, looking for specific behaviors consistent with workshop content the teacher identifies.
• View videotapes with staff members.
• Review lesson plans.
• Facilitate opportunities for staff members to observe each other.

In addition to participants' positive feedback, we often see examples of how professional growth has affected day-to-day classroom operations. Sometimes we hear the language of the new learning in meetings and planning sessions. At other times, we see the new learning reflected in daily curriculum planning. Students and parents often describe classroom projects and events that reflect workshop content.

*   *   *

The staff development model described in this chapter has proved highly effective for our school. In our day-to-day operations, we see examples of many students and staff members processing information differently. The habits of mind are frequently used and recommended as a course of action when someone is at a loss for what to do next.

Every day we see how the habits of mind have been infused into the school's culture. Workshop participants increasingly take responsibility for their own learning, and they now come to the sessions with specific implementation goals in mind. They are willing to discuss approaches and eager to pose questions. They expect to work, and they are willing to take risks while practicing strategies. This process has helped us create a culture that embraces the philosophy of continuous improvement and growth.

Our miniworkshop model has served as a vehicle for meaningful growth for all professionals. The model considers individual differences in learning styles, needs, and background information. The miniworkshops provide not only information and modeling, but also a secure setting for guided practice, time for implementation, and an opportunity for follow-up and coaching.

Our model provides an intimate environment for in-depth collegial dialogue. The professional connections made during these miniworkshops strengthen our staff as a whole. Staff members experience learning from a recipient's point of view, and they can then use those experiences to strengthen the learning environment in their classrooms. This model may seem labor-intensive or expensive because of the size of our groups; however, the size encourages a deeper learning and more opportunity for dialogue.

In actuality, we only use a small amount of building staff development funds to support this program, and we obtain grants from many sources to cover the majority of the costs. The money spent is more than offset by the depth of content we can provide, the strengthening of collegial relationships, the impact on our building environment, and the visible implementation of critical thinking skills and strategies.

Teacher beliefs are at the heart of reform efforts in schools. For changes in words and deeds to occur, teachers must first believe these new behaviors are worthy. Beliefs are shaped by experiences. When teachers and other staff members experience new ways of teaching and learning within an environment where risk taking and experimentation are valued, we advance the prospects for success regarding the implementation of new ways of being, and, in the process, promote success for all learners.

Robbins, 1998

REFERENCES

Costa, A. (1991a). *The school as a home for the mind*. Palatine, IL: SkyLight Publishers.

Costa, A. (Ed.). (1991b). *Developing minds: A resource book for teaching thinking* (Rev. ed., Vol. 1). Alexandria, VA: Association for Supervision and Curriculum Development.

Robbins, P. (1998, September 24). *One new vision for staff development*. Learning packet presented at a workshop sponsored by The Wisconsin Staff Development Council, Brookfield, WI.

BIBLIOGRAPHY

Daresh, J. C. (1987, March). Lessons from research: Staff development: Guidelines for the principal. *NASSP Bulletin 71*(497), 20–23.

Hansen, D. J. (1993). *The relationship between teachers' perceptions of staff development, career stage, and job satisfaction: A thesis submitted to the faculty of the graduate school of the University of Minnesota.*

Joyce, B. R., Hersh, R. H., & McKibbin, M. (1983). *The structure of school improvement*. New York: Longman, Inc.

Joyce, B., & Showers, B. (1980, February). Improving inservice training: The messages of research. *Educational Leadership 37*(5), 375–385.

Lambert, L. (1989, September). The end of an era of staff development. *Educational Leadership 47*(1), 78–81.

Moffett, C. (1989, September). Responses to Lambert: How do we get there from here? *Educational Leadership 47*(1), 82.

Sparks, G. M. (1983, November). Synthesis of research on staff development for effective teaching. *Educational Leadership 41*(3), 65–72.

5

SHARING A WEALTH
OF KNOWLEDGE
AND EXPERIENCE

ARTHUR L. COSTA AND BENA KALLICK

I can't understand why people are frightened by new ideas. I'm frightened of old ones.

John Cage

As school and district personnel become aware of the value of the habits of mind, they also become curious about what they must do to begin the learning journey toward implementation. This chapter considers some of the most frequently asked questions about implementing the habits of mind.

In Chapter 1, we identified seven indicators that can be used to evaluate a school's progress as it becomes a home for the mind. But those indicators are just the road signs on a school's journey. How can a school begin the trip? How should staff members support the travel? What happens on the day-to-day trek toward building a school that is a home for the mind?

Organized around the seven indicators, this chapter draws from several learning journeys of schools and districts that have successfully implemented the habits of mind. Because there is no single answer to any question and no best way of working, we offer the knowledge and experiences of these educators:

• John Kiemele, former principal, Raleigh Hills Elementary School, Beaverton, Oregon.

48

• Alan Cooper, former headmaster, St. George's School, Wanganui, New Zealand.

• Donna Norton Swindal, former resource teacher, Hidden Valley Elementary School and Edward N. Neill Elementary School, Burnsville, Minnesota.

• Angie Chock, reading resource teacher, Royal Elementary School, Honolulu, Hawaii.

• Fred Morton, superintendent of schools, Montgomery County, Virginia.

• Stephen Gasken, principal, Danbury High School, Danbury, Texas.

• Rick Wilhelm, principal, West Orchard Elementary School, Chappaqua, New York.

• Educators at three agencies in Eau Claire, Wisconsin:

° Eau Claire Area School District, represented by Laurie Hittman, executive director of instructional services and chair of the Eau Claire District Critical Thinking Leadership Team.

° Meadowview Elementary School, represented by the Critical Thinking Leadership Team: Ilene Doty, principal; Gerry Holt, teacher; Mary Kay Kopf, teacher; Karen Hirsch, resource teacher; and Laurie Hittman (executive director of instructional services, Eau Claire Area School District).

° DeLong Middle School, represented by Deborah Hansen, coordinator of staff development.

The questions are organized under the seven indicators:

• Shared vision, outcomes, and goals.
• Curriculum, instruction, and assessment.
• School culture.
• Communication and collaboration.
• Leadership.
• Resourceful school community.
• Continuous learning.

You can scan the questions and choose the ones that most interest you. As your interests change, you may want to return to the questions for additional insights and answers.

INDICATOR 1:
SHARED VISION, OUTCOMES, AND GOALS

How does a vision become shared?

In the vignettes below, we see how three different schools began their learning journeys by working with a vision of the habits of mind. Each school first gathered information about the habits of mind, but then their visions evolved differently. Despite these differences, there is an obvious commonality in their commitment to the habits of mind.

HIDDEN VALLEY ELEMENTARY SCHOOL
(From Donna Norton Swindal)

The subcommittee on thinking, composed of the principal, teachers, and parents, began its work with information gathering. They read numerous documents about the habits of mind, performed an ERIC search, listened to Arthur Costa's tapes on the habits, attended a conference to hear Harvard's David Perkins speak on Smart Schools, participated in seminars about multiple intelligences, and visited the classrooms of nearby schools that had adopted the habits of mind.

Eventually, our staff development director presented a summary of the habits of mind to the staff. At another meeting, the principal of a nearby school shared what the habits of mind meant to him personally and professionally. He also described how he used the habits of mind to coach staff and students.

The subcommittee on thinking decided that the habits of mind were the most user-friendly approach they'd seen. They also decided that the habits were valuable because all students could easily understand them and use them to enhance their success. The subcommittee proposed a vision to the whole-site council, faculty, and PTO. Staff members and parents in those groups decided that they would like to see the habits of mind used in the school.

Eventually, the following vision statement was adopted: "Hidden Valley Elementary is committed to establishing a respectful learning environment where educational opportunities promote learning for today and tomorrow. The partnership between students, staff, parents, and the community focuses on maximizing each student's potential through a climate of effective thinking." From this vision came the slogan "Success for All Learners Through Effective Thinking." From then on, Hidden Valley dubbed the teaching and using of the habits of mind as "Effective Thinking."

RALEIGH HILLS ELEMENTARY SCHOOL

(From John Kiemele)

When we decided to work with the habits of mind, I rounded up the entire teaching staff, put us on a school bus, and took off to learn about Arthur Costa's "School as a Home for the Mind" (Costa, 1991). After this presentation, we worked hard to put to paper our ideas about what we wanted students to learn in school, a task much easier said than done. Eventually, the entire Raleigh Hills staff gathered together with selected parents and a few central office administrators to generate a practical vision for Raleigh Hills.

Our next step was to discuss roadblocks that might prevent us from achieving our desired outcomes. Yet we did not accept just any barrier. For example, we did not allow "insufficient funding" as a reason for not being able to achieve our vision. This guideline helped us stretch our thinking and brainstorm creative solutions to the potential bumps in the road.

The next major component was to develop a strategic directions matrix in which we examined each obstacle and generated ideas to overcome it. Using this matrix made the vision we created truly practical.

The final component in our school planning process was to design a system to assess progress and explain our efforts to the community and district. Thus, the practical vision was developed by consensus (a critical group process factor), served as the recorded agreement, and became the plan that guided our efforts to become a more intelligent learning organization. These plans were evaluated and revised as necessary to fine-tune our activities and strategies in the context of our ever-changing community and student needs.

ST. GEORGE'S SCHOOL

(From Alan Cooper)

The St. George's approach was never a carefully detailed strategic plan or a carefully structured pattern. Yet our approach was not chaos, either. The motivating factor was the idea itself, given that the teachers were working in a school culture that cherished change and risk taking.

The idea of the habits of mind was introduced in a formal staff professional development session. They were then implemented across the school to the degree that each teacher felt comfortable with them. Their use was monitored by informal discussion and more formal teacher portfolios.

We decided that the best strategy was on-the-job learning: learning by actually using the habits of mind as part of the curriculum delivery. Thus, students and teachers would learn together. This system required teachers to believe strongly that what they did made a difference. They were interested and involved because of this intrinsic belief in themselves. They focused on experimenting with new ideas and how those ideas could make a difference. They followed ideas, not leaders.

Because St. George's teachers are self-moderating, self-critical, and always on the lookout to do better, they usually are discontented with the status quo. In such a culture, the teachers seek improvements through a whole group of solutions that connect and interlock on a wide front. They reject panacea-type answers that are always going to be insufficient on their own and, ultimately, disappointing. Teachers share an ongoing dialogue about how habits of mind, learning styles, and Thinking Maps® interact with and affect students' motivation, skill development, and competence. In the course of this work, teachers demonstrate an integrity where they, their students, and students' parents learn together, constantly observing and reflecting on their own actions to ensure continuous improvement. The school becomes a learning organization through its own momentum.

INDICATOR 2:
CURRICULUM, INSTRUCTION, AND ASSESSMENT

How are the habits of mind integrated into a curriculum?

Following are two interesting examples of integrating the habits of mind into the curriculum. These descriptions also illustrate very different decision-making processes. The first is a more structured and focused approach; the second, more evolutionary and varied.

EAU CLAIRE AREA SCHOOL DISTRICT

(From Laurie Hittman)

Officials of the Eau Claire Area School District invited community members and educators to participate in strategic planning to emphasize critical thinking and moral responsibility throughout the educational environment. Team members agreed that the habits of mind should not be taught in isolation; they should be integrated into the entire educational process. We strongly believed that if school personnel model the habits of mind, students are more likely to use critical thinking. Thus, we established critical thinking as a fundamental ground rule for all our discussions and interaction.

One of our major goals was to consistently and purposefully integrate critical thinking in the preK–12 curriculum. Here is what we did:

• Developed and demonstrated model lessons in classrooms.
• Created checklists for grades 4 and 5 to assess critical thinking.
• Developed and shared sample lesson plans incorporating the habits of mind in written form.
• Appointed curriculum committees with teachers who have been involved in staff development related to critical thinking.
• Chose instructional strategies and resources that support critical thinking and promote divergent points of view.
• Fostered the ongoing integration of subject areas around broad themes or questions based on an inquiry approach.
• Developed standards for the preK–12 curriculum to help teachers assess students' critical thinking.
• Created a packet for beginning teachers to provide information on critical thinking.

We have made significant progress during the last seven years, systematically implementing critical thinking and the habits of mind. Because these goals are complex and the instructional changes are difficult to implement, we need to provide continued support and leadership during the next 7 to 10 years for maximum integration of critical thinking in the district.

St. George's School

(From Alan Cooper)

The vision at St. George's School focused on preparation for lifelong learning, adaptability and flexibility in problem solving, and the willingness to work with others. These goals were integrated into a strong numeracy and literacy base. In essence, our vision was to produce an efficacious person who would be comfortable when faced by any paradox. We also had to find a practical way of introducing skills and processes that would nestle within New Zealand's curriculum requirements. Such integration was a major determinant in the way we eventually adopted both the habits of mind and David Hyerle's work with thinking skills.

For example, when students in the science class were given a data-collection task, perhaps using a circle map, the teacher would use the overhead projector to show a complete list of data. Students would then check their list against the teacher's model. The explicit nature of the habits of mind was introduced at this stage. Before checking from the overhead projection model, the students would consult large charts marked with the catchwords of "The Intelligent Dozen." These charts listed the habits of mind as we defined them. The students would then tell the teacher what habit of mind they were practicing.

We introduced the habits of mind schoolwide, but each class used different methods. One class laminated a series of guides describing specific actions that indicated an intelligence was being used. Assembly time reinforced various intelligences through stories and real-life examples. Soon, the intelligences were internalized, and they became an integral part of the school culture.

INDICATOR 3:
SCHOOL CULTURE

How are the habits of mind built into district policies and practices? How do they become the school's norms?

The following two vignettes answer the first question and illustrate how the habits of mind are infused into two school personnel functions: hiring and evaluating teachers. The third vignette illustrates one possible answer to the second question. Supporting the habits of mind in policies and practice goes a long way toward building them into the culture of the school, but the habits must also eventually become the school's norms.

DANBURY HIGH SCHOOL
(From Stephen Gasken)

One of the major roles of our site-based committee is to hire new staff whose beliefs and teaching approaches are aligned with our overall school vision. As a committee, we have developed a set of interview questions we ask all potential employees in the interview process. These questions spark specific responses related directly to our vision. The specific habits of mind we look for are

- Persisting.
- Listening with understanding and empathy.
- Questioning and posing problems.
- Thinking about thinking (metacognition).
- Finding humor.

Here are examples of questions we ask and the process we use:

- "Describe a situation in which you used the skill of persistence in your current or last position. What did you do?"
- "Describe what you would do to solve this problem: You have just been assigned to teach a new AP class and quickly realize that you have

more 'regular' students in the class than AP students. What would you do to meet the needs of these students?"

• "Describe the attributes or characteristics of a good listener. What does a good listener do?"

• "What are some examples of how you have used humor to cope with the everyday grind of your job?"

• "The last part of the interview will allow you to pose specific questions to the committee. Take as much time as you need to formulate your questions. We will answer them to the best of our ability."

As we evaluate candidates, we consider the time they take to process their questions, if they write them down, and the quality of the questions. After they have completed this part of the interview, we ask them to describe their thinking: "When we informed you that you would have the opportunity to ask questions, describe the process you used to formulate your questions."

WEST ORCHARD ELEMENTARY SCHOOL
(From Rick Wilhelm)

Figure 5.1 (see pp. 56–57) contains my evaluation report of teacher Lisa Davis using the district's teacher evaluation form and process. This report shows how I look for the habits of mind in a lesson. The report also illustrates how I communicate my value of the habits of mind and how I support the teacher's work with the habits.

ST. GEORGE'S SCHOOL
(From Alan Cooper)

As St. George's continued its work with the habits of mind, teachers learned alongside their students, and they all were engaged in practicing the same sort of habits of mind. In particular, their own metacognition and risk taking were crucial to the success.

Teachers were encouraged to work in teams to mentor each other. Students' and parents' input was also included. In this way, ideas were developed, tested, and refined in a cooperative, friendly, and nonthreatening manner. Most important, these processes helped turn the school into a true learning organization. Our students are now starting to keep portfolios as well, which will soon give further detail to the assessment picture.

Many forms of celebration reinforced the worth of what was happening in the classroom: a simple demonstration for the principal, a "corridor conference" where colleagues shared their successes, and a one-minute

FIGURE 5.1
A "Mindful" Evaluation

WEST ORCHARD ELEMENTARY SCHOOL
Observation Report

Teacher: Lisa Davis   **Date:** 5/9/97
Observer: Rick Wilhelm   **Time:** 10:10 a.m.
Class: 4th grade   **Conference:** 5/12/97

Lesson Summary: At the beginning of the observation period, the class was discussing a problem involving two race cars, one 24 cm. long and the other 12 cm.,
traveling on the same track at the same speed. The question posed was, Which one
won? Ideas ranged from a tie to one or the other car winning. As the discussion
was approaching an end, one boy continued to explain why he thought it had to
be a tie. Another child presented him with a button as a reward for being persist-
ent, a habit of mind featured in the class. Many of the children asked the teacher to
give the answer. She asked that they be patient and wait for the end of the day
because there would be a connection with the math lesson. She asked the class to
look for the connection.

A transition to the math lesson was initiated by asking for a definition of probability. Several ideas were ventured, including estimating and the chance that something will happen. The example of a coin toss was presented with the question,
"What's the chance of getting heads when I flip this coin?" Answers were followed
with the presentation of a scale with the extremes of "never" and "always." The
teacher asked, "What in your life can you always count on happening, and what can
you know will never happen? Talk with your partner." A variety of ideas were generated and presented table by table. As each was discussed, it became apparent that
it was difficult to reach an agreement. The teacher noted this point.

Returning to the scale, the class was asked to label more points along the continuum at the quarter mark, the middle, and the three-quarter mark. They chose
"usually," "sometimes," and "rarely." The teacher asked which was a better chance of
getting a six, rolling a die or drawing a numbered tile from a bucket with many such
tiles with different numbers. A boy responded that the die was most likely because
there were fewer numbers on it than there were in the bucket.

Next, two class members were asked to come up for a demonstration. One
was given a die with all sixes and the other was a standard die. With six rolls of the
dice, the results were compared for how many sixes were drawn. When the difference in the dice was discovered, the class declared it unfair. The teacher then asked
what was fair. Two children came up to demonstrate a method that they considered fair, using the same dice. The teacher showed the class a bag with five green
tiles and five yellow tiles, asking what the chances were for pulling out a green tile.
One child thought it was 1 in 10 and another, 1 in 2. The teacher asked if one pull
from the bag would be fair. Five pulls were suggested. With one yellow tile out of
the bag, the teacher asked if it was fair now. It was decided that it wouldn't be fair,
and the class considered how fairness might be promoted with different methods.

FIGURE 5.1—*continued*
A "Mindful" Evaluation

Finally, directions were given to groups, arranged by table, for an experiment. Each group was given a bag with three red tiles, one yellow, and one blue. To draw a tile, students must first shake the bag. Each group member would take a turn at drawing a tile. Results for 20 turns were to be recorded with tally marks on a sheet and then translated into a percent and a fraction. Before beginning, each group was to predict how many times out of 20 a red tile would be pulled. The groups proceeded to follow the directions.

Administrator's Comments: This lesson was an excellent example of an inductive approach to the complex topic of probability. You drew the class into the concept of chance with the coin toss and dice. From there you led them to a consideration of the concept of fairness, and then to the elements of a good design for an experiment with probability. In each part of the lesson, you kept the thinking open by not confirming or giving the answers: "We couldn't really agree. Is it fair? So you think it's 1 out of 10, and you think it's 1 out of 2." The children have learned that not only will you facilitate their thinking, but they must also rely on their own powers of reason to find answers. They accept the idea that you will not interfere in their thinking. This is a major accomplishment and requires an extremely supportive classroom environment where taking a risk is valued by all. The evidence that such an environment exists in your class is that students acknowledge each other when a risk is taken and it's celebrated. The same is true for other habits of mind such as persistence and being precise. The level of active participation was high as you invited the class into the consideration of problems. Several techniques were employed during this lesson, such as talking to a partner, discussing as a table group, and explaining to the whole class. In spite of the energy and enthusiasm displayed in the period, you could bring the class to a focus with signals that were quickly received and responded to. In addition, you wove into the lesson your high expectations for evidence to support thoughts ("Raise your hand and be prepared to defend. . . . Is that specific enough? Think about it").

You successfully engaged the students in the complexities of probability with examples that were very appropriate for their developmental levels. The result will be a more integrated and complete understanding. Great lesson! I enjoyed watching an expert at work.

Teacher	Administrator
Date	Date

Source: Rick Wilhelm, West Orchard Elementary School, Chappaqua, New York.

update at the weekly staff meeting where teachers shared with other teachers a success from their classroom.

Parents have to be a part of the implementation and reinforcement if the school is to be a true learning organization. St. George's held parent forums and distributed a simple booklet about the habits of mind. This booklet helped parents become aware of the practical application of the habits of mind at home.

Never underestimate the power of teacher modeling. When teachers model thinking skills by using Thinking Maps on the chalkboard, in classroom wall displays, and in their own planning and reporting, they are giving an authenticity to the activity by affirming that adults too use the skills students are being taught. This affirmation promotes a kind of integrity. When we talk about lifelong learning, or how the habits of mind are superior skills to have and to use, we validate those statements by using the skills ourselves. Both students and parents notice this congruence, too.

INDICATOR 4:
COMMUNICATION AND COLLABORATION

How can the habits of mind be spread to other schools within the district? To parents? Throughout the community?

Students need to encounter the habits of mind continuously throughout their education. The home and community should also reflect the value of using the habits of mind. The following anecdotes describe how several schools have worked toward these goals.

EAU CLAIRE AREA SCHOOL DISTRICT

(From Laurie Hittman)

Many members of the school district have taken classes and workshops in critical thinking, and they are working toward creating a critical thinking environment in their classrooms. We have found that the collaboration of district administrators, building principals, classroom teachers, and the parent community creates a solid foundation for progress in critical thinking.

HIDDEN VALLEY ELEMENTARY SCHOOL

(From Donna Norton Swindal)

In a workshop before school began, we explained the long-term overview of the year's plan. Throughout the year, we taught staff members the habits of mind during a 25- to 30-minute "core course" at each bimonthly staff meeting. The teachers were then to teach the habits to the students within the next two weeks. Each teacher was asked to send a letter home to parents introducing them to that behavior. As a facilitator team, our consultant, Marlene Honerman, and I would be available to support teachers in their classrooms by modeling lessons, team teaching, and helping plan how to weave the habits of mind into the curriculum.

We determined to model a good teaching strategy each time we presented a habit. Teachers began with a "carousel" activity to describe what effective thinking might look or sound like. We closed the lesson by leading a reflection on which habits of mind were used in the activity, and we gave each teacher a classroom poster listing the habits we used.

We celebrated what we had accomplished, and we shared the successes we saw in classrooms. At year's end, the whole school celebrated because we had internalized seven habits in the first year. We played special interviews and news summaries on our intranet television station. Students seemed to find joy in the process. One class, with the assistance of our music teacher, wrote and performed a song about the habits of mind. Another class wrote a rap. Our kitchen staff, who helped us practice the habits of mind all year, made special "Effective Thinking" cookies for the whole school.

By the end of two years, all the habits of mind had been taught to the whole staff and, consequently, to students. During the second year, the Hidden Valley Effective Thinking Committee also developed lessons to provide inservice sessions for each year's new, certified teachers, and for all new building staff members, including educational assistants, management paraprofessionals, cooks, custodians, office workers, and health staff. Now, students would hear about the habits of mind from every direction.

*   *   *

A core group of supportive parents helped recruit other parents to assist in implementing the habits of mind. The first parent committee created "Effective Thinking Home Sheets" for each habit of mind. The expectation was that teachers would teach the behavior to their students and then send home a sheet to the parents to follow up and support the teachers' work.

The parent committee set up parent inservice evenings on such topics as "What is Thinking?", "Writing as a Tool for Thinking," and "Multiple Intelligences/Multiple Learning Styles." One parent used her artistic talents to develop large banners about the habits of mind for the building's entrance hall. A father used his artistic skills to develop four-panel cartoons featuring his daughter and her dog in a kind of "Calvin and Hobbes" look at life for each of the habits of mind.

MEADOWVIEW ELEMENTARY SCHOOL

(From Ilene Doty)

To help parents become familiar with critical thinking, we offered informational meetings in the evenings and at lunchtime. The staff developed a "Luggage for Literature" project to connect the habits of mind, the district's health curriculum, and literature. We purchased briefcase bags to send home with students. Each bag contains a writing journal; a storybook; and laminated cards that describe the habits of mind, one health-related issue, and ideas to generate parent-and-child discussion. Every classroom has 15 bags available for students to take home for reading, writing, and discussion.

HIDDEN VALLEY ELEMENTARY SCHOOL

(From Donna Norton Swindal)

Hidden Valley teachers met with local business leaders to acquaint them with the habits of mind. We also encouraged these adults to visit the school to tell students how they used the habits in their daily work. Many businesses we contacted responded enthusiastically. One company, B.F. Goodrich Rosemount Aerospace, even allowed students to tour their plant to see how the habits of mind can be used in a variety of settings. The company also made its staff members aware of the habits before the children's visit.

MEADOWVIEW ELEMENTARY SCHOOL

(From Ilene Doty)

As they became familiar with the habits of mind and began to value their usefulness, students wondered how the habits could be applied in the broader community. The students' interest in sharing their new knowledge prompted a lengthy discussion. The students decided that they would like to write informative speeches to present to community members.

Twenty-six students worked in pairs using the habits of mind. They presented their speeches at the Eau Claire City Council, Royal Credit Union Board of Directors, and a meeting of district administrators. The students have also discussed the possibility of speaking about the habits of mind at an Eau Claire School Board meeting.

ROYAL ELEMENTARY SCHOOL

(From Angie Chock)

As we reached out to the Royal Elementary School community, we tried to model the habits of mind in our efforts to gain their understanding and support. Here are some of our strategies and the habits they reinforce:

• Invite community members to special school events so they can wonder at the awesome things you're doing at school. (Responding with wonderment and awe)

• Build awareness by welcoming the community into your school. (Responding with wonderment and awe)

• Show enthusiasm for your work and belief in your vision. (Responding with wonderment and awe)

• Listen to your community partners for great suggestions, good input, and a different point of view. (Listening with understanding and empathy)

• Be precise in asking for what you want. Refer to your action plan. (Thinking and communicating with clarity and precision)

• Give specific directions, and assign roles for your community volunteers. (Thinking and communicating with clarity and precision)

• Assess and reflect on the role of your community in your school and the participation of your school in your community. (Thinking about thinking [metacognition])

• Be open to suggestions from a community group even though its members may not be able to fulfill your needs exactly. They may offer you other options. (Thinking flexibly)

• Brainstorm with community groups to develop activities tailored to your school's needs. (Thinking flexibly)

• Use the resources within your school to help you network with "friends of friends." (Applying past knowledge to new situations)

• Ask for help from other organizations if one organization is unable to help you at the time you need help. That first organization may be of help at another time. Ask again, especially if they have expressed interest in assisting you. (Persisting)

• Persevere in finding community groups that will work best for and within your school. (Persisting)

• Show the community your resolve through the commitment and participation of your parents, students, and school employees in school activities. (Persisting)

• Be sure community volunteers know what is expected of them. (Striving for accuracy)

• Provide a liaison between your school and each community group that works with the school to assure that the correct instructions and requests are relayed. (Striving for accuracy)

• Ask for help. Many service organizations will offer their assistance. (Questioning and posing problems)

• Be selective in the kinds of activities your school participates in with the community. Think about how those activities reflect your school's vision. (Managing impulsivity)

• Brainstorm new directions and new ideas with your community partners. (Creating, imagining, innovating)

INDICATOR 5:
LEADERSHIP

How do leaders support habits of mind?

The habits of mind are more effectively implemented when a school is influenced by strong leadership. Such influence does not necessarily mean that the building principal or district superintendent is responsible for leadership; rather, it means that someone in the school or district is the cheerleader for the habits of mind. This cheerleading can come in many forms: making formal presentations, leading discussions, finding materials, cajoling, encouraging, and, most important, modeling. Consider the following examples.

HIDDEN VALLEY ELEMENTARY SCHOOL
(From Donna Norton Swindal)

Our principal and assistant principal attended and participated in every core course and workshop meeting about the habits of mind. They attended evening sessions for parents and helped with grant writing. When the staff and I saw that kind of commitment, we couldn't help but be enthusiastic about what we were doing.

ST. GEORGE'S SCHOOL
(From Alan Cooper)

Implementation for teachers was clearly and simply on-the-job training and practical application within the normal classroom day. Although I would cajole and gently prod, my main role was to act as a colleague and mentor. By taking classes and trying out the new processes, I modeled what was required of other staff. Sometimes I collaborated with a teacher; sometimes I worked with a class on my own. Sometimes there would be failure when working with another teacher's class, but the teacher would modify and improve to change the failure into success. The autonomy of each teacher was essential to continual improvement.

RALEIGH HILLS ELEMENTARY SCHOOL

(From John Kiemele)

I would frequently remind the teachers about the habits of mind through the weekly school bulletin (see Figure 5.2). I also made regular morning announcements about the habit of mind "Target for the Week." This was an easy way to coach the faculty in their efforts to create learning opportunities where habits of mind could be reinforced.

FIGURE 5.2
Principal's Bulletin

September 15–19, 1997
Alpha Week on the Master Schedule
Patrol Assignment: Squad A
Lunch Helpers: Mrs. Gilroy's Class
Bus Duty: Grade 4 Team

Intelligent Behavior Target: Striving for Accuracy and Precision

Students may often be careless when completing and turning in their work. The speed of getting the job done may surpass the child's desire for achieving craftsmanship. This week, be sure to provide your students with models that you expect them to follow in completing assignments and tasks. Do they know your expectations clearly? Are the children aware of the criteria you will use and that they need to employ in order to submit a satisfactory product? Try to orally reinforce the students whom you observe to check and recheck their assignments and use those experiences as teachable moments for the class as a whole.

Source: Raleigh Hills Elementary School, Beaverton, Oregon.

MONTGOMERY COUNTY

(From Fred Morton)

Entering a new district is a little like the story in the movie *The Gods Must Be Crazy.* As you may recall, a tribal person living in a primitive setting was totally puzzled when a soda bottle fell from the sky. The bottle was so alien to his culture that he built all sorts of interpretations as to what the bottle was and why it was sent. Likewise, coming into a district as superintendent is a bit like being the bottle falling into an existing culture. The good news is that you have an opportunity to rethink the way the culture operates. The bad news is that everyone is suspicious about what you are up to.

63

Here is the process I developed for introducing the habits of mind to my administrative team:

1. Give everyone a description of the habits of mind. Ask people to read it before coming to the first meeting.

2. At the first meeting, ask everyone to rank the top two habits that they feel are their strength and the two habits they feel they really need to work on.

3. Ask participants to chart their list of strengths publicly, with a group member creating the chart on a large paper on the wall.

4. Without discussion, end the meeting with the chart on the wall.

5. At the second meeting, ask each participant to rank the top two habits that they perceived each member of the team most frequently displayed. (These colleagues had worked together for many years, and they operated in an atmosphere of trust and collegiality.) These habits are also charted for each person.

6. For the third meeting, print the chart, and give people the opportunity to study the list. When my team did this, they analyzed their self-perceptions in relation to the perceptions of their teammates. They also raised questions about meaning. For example, a person who was rated high for using the habit of striving for accuracy wanted to know what people meant by that. This conversation provided an opportunity for this person to get some feedback about how well he serves the group by that exact behavior, a behavior that he felt was sometimes not well received among the more global thinkers!

7. At the last meeting, analyze areas of strength that the entire team as a whole represents. Invite team members to talk about what actions they will take based on their insights.

The analysis of the charts was guided by the following questions:

- What do the habits mean to me?
- What do the habits mean to the team?
- What do the habits mean about me to other people?

INDICATOR 6:
RESOURCEFUL SCHOOL COMMUNITY

How are resources of time, energy, and finances located and mobilized?

Commitment to the habits of mind means a commitment to allocating a school's most precious resources: time, energy, and finances. Consider how the following school devoted all three resources to support their work with the habits of mind.

HIDDEN VALLEY ELEMENTARY SCHOOL

(From Donna Norton Swindal)

Staff members voted to commit all of the next year's staff development monies for the building to create one full-time specialist position for an "effective thinking facilitator." Additional funds were designated for supplies and outside consultants.

The role of effective thinking facilitator invented itself as the year progressed. This staff member codeveloped and taught all the habits of mind workshops and core courses. She developed and taught many units of study for grades K–6 in math, language arts, science, music, and art. The goal was always to teach the subject area in depth while weaving in the habits of mind.

The facilitator acted as an on-site resource for teachers. She posted notes and projects in the lounge, shared references from the literature, circulated teacher materials and ideas, and acted as an in-building support person. She worked with colleagues who requested assistance through modeling, team teaching, or observation of lessons or short units of study. The facilitator worked with two parent committees and led four evening seminars for parents. Other duties included organizing a grant committee to gain more funding and developing a longitudinal assessment study.

INDICATOR 7:
CONTINUOUS LEARNING

How are data collected?
How do the data inform us about the effects of our experimentation?

Effective schools gather data to assess the effects of experimentation. In this section, we draw upon the experiences of three schools that have ventured into experimentation, data gathering, and interpretation of those data.

HIDDEN VALLEY ELEMENTARY SCHOOL

(From Donna Norton Swindal)

We observed that students automatically elaborated and explained their answers as they gave them. There were fewer disciplinary trips to the office. By videotaping students in small groups, we collected evidence of how they applied the habits of mind to their problem solving.

When I was in the lunchroom, or when I passed colleagues in the halls, they would quickly relate comments from students or their parents that showed how our habits of mind were being used or interpreted. From time to time, teachers would send me a student who had just made a good connection in class. The student would then repeat the connection to me.

Parents, too, would call me, feeling more efficacious about their parenting because they had first listened with empathy and understanding and therefore felt that they provided their child with a more level-headed response to a given situation. One parent even called to say she had helped her child with homework by quoting information we sent home about applying previous knowledge to new situations.

St. George's School

(From Alan Cooper)

In keeping with the teacher's freedom to experiment, some teachers are starting to construct rubrics, both for themselves and for students. These, like the portfolios, show where students are coming from, where they are now, and where they will go next. Later, these portfolios will be consolidated into a whole school template.

St. George's also uses less formal anecdotal assessments from parent feedback. For example, a parent discussed bad behavior with a child, and the child articulated the need to be less impulsive. The parent expressed surprise to the teacher that his 10-year-old could not only describe such concepts but also understood them as well!

Parents, especially those in managerial and marketing jobs, report using in their workplaces some of the thinking skills and processes taught to their children. Such situations are quite clearly the parent learning from the child. In one sense, the process is remarkable; in another, the result is a logical part of the learning organization concept.

The bridge between implementation and assessment is our use of rubrics for teacher professional development. By using the novice-to-expert model, teachers are able to see where they have come from, where they are now, and where they need to go next. This approach nestles neatly into performance appraisal as well. Staff members, however, need to understand that learning is seldom linear. Slavishly following a rubric is counterproductive.

The teacher's portfolio is a key assessment item. This portfolio is a record detailing a teacher's journey over time. To guide their work with these portfolios, St. George's teachers are developing their own rubrics based on the novice-to-expert model. The portfolios' greatest importance as a means of assessment is how they empower. The teacher clearly has the ownership and control, selecting the scope of the portfolio and the artifacts to be displayed in it.

RALEIGH HILLS ELEMENTARY SCHOOL

(From John Kiemele)

The staff sincerely believed that by modeling, coaching, and even explicitly teaching these habits of mind consistently, students could reach high levels of thinking, learning, and achievement. Between designing and following our schoolwide plans and agreeing on common indicators of desired student dispositions, the staff was able to identify a multitude of strategies and situations that would foster the desired student behaviors throughout the school. Our speech pathologist, for example, found ways to help students who met with her for therapy foster the habits of mind in games and activities.

Evidence of the effectiveness of our experiment was collected through notes, student samples, and teacher testimonies. For example, a library instructional aide reported:

> Dear John: During this morning's Junior Great Books session with Mrs. [Smith's] students we had a "measurable moment." We were discussing the "reputation" of a character using vocabulary words from the story when several students connected the terms to being impulsive!

This note was sent to me from a primary grade teacher:

> One of my 1st graders had been spending a three-day weekend at her grandparent's farm. On Saturday afternoon, Grandpa asked if she wanted to watch him chop down a tree. She excitedly said, "Yes!" Armed with his trusty ax, Grandpa began to hack at the trunk of a rather large evergreen. His granddaughter was anxious to see the big tree fall. After watching Grandpa chop at the tree for almost 30 minutes without success, [Jan] with her hands perched firmly on her hips, said, "Grandpa, I think you are going to need a lot more perseverance and a lot bigger ax!"

*   *   *

The distribution and collection of comments gathered from numerous parental surveys were critical components of our action research. In the spring of 1998, one such survey created by parents, teachers, and support staff was distributed to each family. In addition to asking for feedback on the overall school program, we specifically asked the parents to rate the value of the staff's emphasis on teaching for intelligence, then to explain their rating. Here is one example of many similar comments:

> I felt that this approach helps children to understand individuality and diversity. I feel the program is valuable for both children *and* adults in understanding different learning styles. I value these qualities [the habits of mind] as an adult and would like to see them expressed in my children. My children have been strongly motivated to enjoy learning. I believe this (program) emphasizes diversity and values the talents of each child. From what I have learned, the Mindful program has taught the kids how to deal with anger better. It has helped me with strategies to improve my own son's learning.

*　　*　　*

In presenting information about our work with the habits of mind to my administrative colleagues and other interested groups outside the school, I was often asked, "How did you analyze what was occurring in the school?" Though I could share numerous observations about the staff and students, quantifying the progress we believed we were making with hard data supplied by a standardized test was difficult.

Then something fascinating occurred. In our school district, 5th graders were administered comprehensive tests of reading and math. The scores are published in the newspaper so the public can compare schools throughout the region. After three years of weaving the habits of mind into our teaching and curriculum, Raleigh Hills' students scored the highest in both reading and math among their elementary peers at 73 other sites.

St. George's School

(From Alan Cooper)

Learning is seldom linear. Progress was uneven especially as different teachers' personalities came into play. Even though the context was the school, the habits of mind were being practiced in real, practical situations. It was much more than learning as an academic exercise in the classroom.

The habits of mind were first raised to the consciousness level and then quite rapidly became part of the total culture of the classroom, school, and working methods. The left-brain period, where the children were still rule-governed and looked for help from the various guides that the teachers employed, was in many cases relatively short. Soon, using the habits became part of the flow and a right-brain activity.

RALEIGH HILLS ELEMENTARY SCHOOL

(From John Kiemele)

When examined as a whole, the positive effects the habits of mind had on the students and staff at Raleigh Hills would be hard to ignore. Taking into account the behaviors we could directly observe in students; reflections shared by teachers over the years; numerous positive comments and perceptions shared by parents, formally and informally; and occasional test data available from traditional sources, I would have to say that our mission was accomplished.

I view these types of learning models as beneficial for all students, because the brain knows no boundaries regarding the economic or cultural background of the learner. I have also seen that powerful learning can occur when teachers truly believe and expect learning to occur. Our vision was realized at Raleigh Hills because of the many staff members and parents who indeed believed that the mind of a child was capable of immeasurable possibilities, and that our students would benefit from the risk we took together to make our school a home for the mind.

MEADOWVIEW ELEMENTARY SCHOOL

(From Ilene Doty)

To teach critical thinking effectively, the habits of mind must become a part of our daily lives. This approach became poignantly apparent when I talked with one of our teachers as she struggled with melanoma. She told me shortly before her death that her attendance in the critical thinking classes and workshops, and the practice of the habits of mind throughout our school, helped her make better medical and life decisions. What better gift to give our students than the kinds of skills you need to make the best possible life decisions?

EAU CLAIRE AREA SCHOOL DISTRICT
MEADOWVIEW ELEMENTARY SCHOOL
DELONG MIDDLE SCHOOL

We are pleased that our district administrators, school principal, and the parents of our children support and encourage our efforts with students. We find it a deeply satisfying experience and well worth the effort to weave critical thinking into our classrooms. The reward is the excitement for learning that we see on our students' faces and in the high quality of their work. The reward is the curiosity we hear in children's questions, the creativity in their answers, and the balance of listening skills and persistence in their discussions.

We observe kids naturally becoming more skilled in the school's core values as they hone their habits of mind. We see them demonstrate intelligent behaviors. We see new connections as the whole school community grows in critical thinking. As professionals, we ourselves have the opportunity to learn and stretch as we work toward improving our own thinking skills. Our reward for all our hard work is in the realization that *this* is the way education is supposed to be!

REFERENCE

Costa, A. (1991). *The school as a home for the mind.* Palatine, IL: SkyLight Publishers.

6

SUSTAINING A FOCUS ON THE HABITS OF MIND

ARTHUR L. COSTA AND BENA KALLICK

Press on. Nothing in the world can take the place of persistence. Talent will not: Nothing is more common than unrewarded talent. Education alone will not: The world is full of educated failures. Persistence alone is omnipotent.

Calvin Coolidge

Inevitably, teachers and administrators find that they have lost sight of their vision of desired educational outcomes. Sometimes educators are temporarily sidetracked by fads, bandwagons, or other educational panaceas. Sometimes they are distracted by pressures from the public and special-interest groups. At other times, educators find their efforts diluted by promising educational innovations that, in the end, have little impact.

Once the habits of mind are well established in a school, they will support significant, thoughtful change in any area. Although educators always need to be open to new approaches and perspectives, they must first make the habits of mind an enduring, essential outcome for their schools. This chapter describes how schools can sustain their focus on the habits of mind to achieve lasting change.

GIVING IT TIME

The habits of mind are not a quick fix. Our experiences in many schools have proved that it takes three to five years to successfully infuse the habits of mind. This process requires well-defined instruction with qualified teachers and carefully constructed curriculum materials. Teachers and administrators will see significant, enduring change in students' behavior only after they make this substantial commitment.

We know that the amount of time on task affects student learning. This relationship is just as true for acquiring thinking skills like the habits of mind. When thinking truly becomes an instructional goal, teachers and administrators will allocate more classroom time for activities in which students learn about, practice, and reflect on cognitive processes.

CONDUCTING ACTION RESEARCH

Many schools focus on action research as a method for continuous examination and improvement. Action research is designed to collect data in the midst of practice. Action research has no control group, as does experimental research. Instead, the researcher defines a series of hypotheses and then collects data to better understand those hypotheses in light of ongoing practice.

Renee Affolter and Frank J. Jacques are two teacher-researchers from Sir Francis Drake High School in San Anselmo, California. They set up studies to determine how the habits of mind might affect their students' work. Affolter focused on the habit of questioning and posing problems. Her study demonstrated that students were far more successful at asking questions related to naming, defining, and describing and less successful with questions that required applying, evaluating, and hypothesizing. As a result, Affolter worked on these questioning skills for herself and her students.

Jacques's study focused on the habit of striving for accuracy. He was concerned that students cared only about performing, not about the content of the performance. He asked his students to demonstrate, record, and reflect on their capability to attend to precision, detail, and revision. He eventually concluded,

> Folding a formal introduction of the concept of "accuracy" into a drawing/painting assignment appears to solicit better product. The overt presentation of the concept establishes an intellectual/behavioral framework that buttresses the art-making activity. It gets students to reflect on the kinesthetic experience and might possibly create a little distance

between the artist and the art making, which can help to diminish inhibition in kids who feel [they] are "inadequate" (personal communication).

Action research provides a powerful structure for studying the habits of mind. The continuous search for new meaning through practice is one of the best ways to keep the habits of mind central to a school's work.

DISCOVERING MORE HABITS

The structure that we have provided in the Habits of Mind series offers a general framework for establishing the habits of mind and building a learning community. As school staff members become more attuned to observing, recording, and analyzing the habits, they probably will do one or more of the following with our original list of habits of mind:

• *Collapse some of the habits into a more concise list.* For example, some groups find that taking responsible risks, thinking flexibly, and finding humor all fit together. Others find that striving for accuracy is similar to thinking and communicating with clarity and precision, and they put the two habits together.

• *Discover that we have overlooked some habits that are significant to their school community.* Adding to the habits and reexamining their meaning in specific contexts sustain the vitality of a staff's work. Each school operates in a specific, constantly changing context; the habits should be adapted to each school's learning community.

• *Consider other habits to add to the list.* For example, "thinking chimerically" might define the ability to imagine and fantasize. (George Lucas would be a fine example of someone who practices this habit.) "Thinking systematically" could be the inclination to find interrelationships and the ability to focus simultaneously on the whole as well as the parts. "Thinking transcendentally" might be the inclination to pose grand, abstract questions (What makes humans human? Why are we here? What is the nature of mankind?).

Our list of the habits of mind is a living document. The list is not meant to be complete or static. Educators should modify, elaborate on, refine, and evaluate the list. Together, we'll all make greater meaning through this process.

BUILDING CONTINUITY

Schools must sustain a focus on the habits of mind throughout a student's educational experience, from elementary through secondary school. Students need to see this continuity of expectations or they, too, fall prey to the "one-year-at a-time" syndrome. Students' learning will be more powerful if they see that schooling is a continuous pattern of learning that rests on the shoulders of the previous year. They gain little if they believe that their education is just a series of isolated episodes.

Work done with the habits of mind in the elementary school must be continued in secondary classes. The most challenging obstacle to this goal is time. Secondary teachers have so much to cover in so little time! Yet those teachers can use that time most efficiently by teaching for several goals simultaneously: content goals, process goals, and the habits of mind.

Content goals are a valuable vehicle for teaching the habits of mind. When teachers use a multilevel approach, students come to understand that experts—scientists, mathematicians, athletes, artists, authors, and historians—are familiar with a vast body of content as well as the dispositions of that discipline. These dispositions invariably include one or more of the habits of mind.

ORIENTING TEACHERS NEW TO THE CULTURE

New teachers make the greatest effort to adapt to a school's culture in the first three years they are there. If the school demonstrates a sharing culture, they will learn how to share. If the habits of mind guide the school's dialogue, new teachers will adapt those habits to their own work. In this context, we are using *new* to refer to both novice and experienced teachers who are new to a school whose culture embraces the habits of mind.

New teachers are more likely to use the habits of mind in their classroom if they see the habits valued and used in other settings. If new teachers hear rhetoric about the habits, but don't see them in daily practice, they'll fear using the habits in their classroom. If new teachers see the habits used in a faculty meeting or parent-teacher conference as well as in other classrooms, they are more likely to use the habits in their own work.

Cultural adaptation is powerful. As mentioned earlier, new teachers can change their value system within the first three years of teaching, using the values of the culture in which they are working (Louis, Marks, & Kruse, 1996). But new teachers cannot necessarily acquire the habits on their own. They must have guidance, see sample instruction, and observe the habits in other classrooms, hallways, and staff meetings and other professional gatherings.

EXTENDING OUR REACH

Staying the course in the midst of a chaotic environment is not easy. Schools need an anchor. We suggest that the habits of mind are such an anchor because they transcend content, programs, and disciplines.

The habits of mind ground a learning community in thoughtful processes. When schools anchor themselves with the habits of mind, they become thoughtful in the fullest sense of the word: sensitive, caring, and full of thought. These goals are why most educators enter the profession. They want to work in a thoughtful environment, to facilitate the thought of their students and their colleagues, and to make the world a more thoughtful place.

If you've read any of the other three books in this series, you won't be surprised when we state that we have a larger, more global agenda for our work. That agenda is to make the world a better place through the habits of mind. We believe that each human being has the drive, potential, and capacity to continually practice and improve in the habits of mind. We further believe that people have the capacities to influence the many communities in which they interact and, therefore, they can make the world a better place.

Many problems plague our world. Each day is filled with economic, social, environmental, scientific, and moral dilemmas, the answers to which are not immediately known. We envision a world that is a continuous learning community where all people are searching for ways to live more harmoniously by thinking interdependently; listening to each other with understanding and empathy; remaining open to continuous learning; persisting; managing impulsivity; and dealing flexibly with the richness of cultural, religious, and human differences.

These changes will take persistence, problem finding, risk taking, and generating increasingly more creative approaches to solving world problems using the habits of mind instead of resorting to the violence, hatred, and war that humans too often use to resolve conflict. To consider just a few of the habits of mind, when we speak of *listening with understanding and empathy*, we are really talking of transcending generations of ethnocentrism to truly see and value the abundant diversity of other cultures, races, religions, language systems, political systems, and economic views to develop a more stable world community.

Thinking about thinking (metacognition) means developing a greater collective consciousness about the effects we have on each other and on the Earth's finite resources so that we can live more respectfully and graciously and in balance with our delicate environment.

We also look to *strive for accuracy* and congruence between our democratic ideals and our decisions and actions, and we strive to *think and communicate with clarity and precision*, regardless of what language others may speak.

We seek to *think interdependently* by caring for and learning from others, helping each other manage Earth's resources in ways that link all humans into a global community.

Alan Kay (1990) says that "the best way to predict the future is to invent it." If we want a future that is much more thoughtful, vastly more cooperative, greatly more compassionate, and a whole lot more loving, then we have to invent it. That future is in our homes, schools, and classrooms today. The habits of mind are the tools we all can use to invent our desired vision of the future.

REFERENCES

Kay, A. (1990, March). *The best way to predict the future is to invent it.* Keynote address presented at the 45th Annual Conference of the Association for Supervision and Curriculum Development, San Francisco, CA.

Louis, K. S., Marks, H. M., & Kruse, S. (1996). Teacher's professional community in restructuring schools. *American Educational Research Journal 33*(4), 757–798.

7

GETTING STARTED

ARTHUR L. COSTA AND BENA KALLICK

This chapter contains a variety of suggestions to further encourage awareness and use of the habits of mind in classrooms, schools, and communities. The list is loosely grouped by topic; we did not use headings because we believed that they might be too limiting. We encourage you to read through and consider each idea.

Some of these ideas may not work for your setting; others may be of great relevance. Your team, group, or staff may wish to rank each item according to the following scale:

- A = Already doing it.
- P = A good possibility.
- M = A must—implement immediately!
- U = Unlikely—it won't fly!

After ranking, develop an action plan to implement the M's, appoint a subcommittee to study the P's, and congratulate yourselves for already doing the A's!

At the end of the chapter, you'll see that the list is purposefully incomplete. Encourage your staff members, students, and community members to brainstorm additions to fit your situation. Although you might be tempted to abandon the U's, save them for a later date. A school's circumstances constantly change, and today's "U" might be tomorrow's "P."

1. Develop a "code of ethics" based on the habits of mind. Distribute this code to every member of the school community. Display the code prominently, and encourage students and staff to refer to the code often. All school policies should reflect this code of ethics.

2. Ensure that the school's recognition and reward systems are based on the habits of mind.

3. Publicly recognize the habits of mind in the work of unsung heroes who keep the school running: custodians, repair staff, secretaries, cafeteria workers, and volunteers.

4. Use the language of the habits of mind in conversations with colleagues.

5. Establish the habits of mind as ground rules for discussions about all practices in the school.

6. Include discussions of the school's "ethos" in faculty meetings and workshops. How might the habits of mind become more apparent in the school's culture?

7. Encourage students and staff to discuss how class rules, school rules, and homework policies reflect and support the habits of mind.

8. When assessing staff development institutes, assess the degree to which the habits of mind were required for the work that was accomplished.

9. Watch for newspaper and magazine cartoons that illustrate one or more of the habits of mind. Display them in the school or classroom, and discuss them with students and staff.

10. Develop a school-year calendar designating one habit of mind to be emphasized per month or week. Suggest activities for parents and teachers to emphasize that habit of mind.

11. Pose the following question in a class or meeting: Can a person be "great" and "good" and still have character flaws?

12. Take a walk through your school with students, staff members, parents, or school officials. Ask them to interpret the school's values based only on their observations of the school environment and student and staff interactions. Where do they see strength in the habits of mind, and where do they see possible areas for improvement?

13. Start a school scrapbook with photos, news stories, and memorabilia reflecting the school's history and accomplishments with the habits of mind. Involve as many school members as possible in contributing to and maintaining the collection. Be sure to share the scrapbook with visitors and new families.

14. Hold a ceremony at the beginning and end of the school year to introduce, recognize, and emphasize the habits of mind.

15. At the conclusion of each faculty or team meeting, place habits of mind "fortunes" in the center of a table. Ask each participant to select a fortune and read it aloud. Here's an example: "Try to understand the other side's point of view. Try to understand other people's views even if you don't agree with them. Such work means giving them an opportunity to explain

their concerns completely so that you can get a clear idea of what's bothering them."

16. Encourage students and staff to draw on the habits of mind to resolve and learn from school or class conflicts.

17. Develop a system of welcoming and orienting new students that emphasizes the habits of mind as the goals and values of your school. When a new student enrolls in the school, welcome the family as well.

18. Describe to students how you use the habits of mind in community service, church work, hobbies, avocations, or sports.

19. Choose a personal motto or mission statement. Share this mission statement with others in the school community. Explain why you chose this motto or mission.

20. Admit your mistakes, and explain how you try to learn from them. Expect—and encourage—students and colleagues to do the same.

21. Illustrate integrity. Let everyone in the school community see that you live out the same expectations of the habits of mind that you place upon them.

22. Institute a student-to-student tutoring program centered around the habits of mind.

23. Promote a schoolwide or intraclass service club. Part of the club's mission should be to infuse the habits of mind in the school, class, or community.

24. Discuss and demonstrate the habits of mind required to care for living creatures. Allow elementary students to take turns caring for class pets, or allow secondary students to care for lab animals in biology class. Also allow students to take the animals home over weekends and holidays.

25. Invite student volunteers to build a playground, pick up litter, plant trees, paint a mural, or remove graffiti. Before and after the event, discuss how the habits of mind play a part in accomplishing a task.

26. Invite students to take responsibility for maintaining and beautifying the school. For example, a class might "adopt a hallway," shelve misplaced library books, or plant flowers. Post signs identifying these special caretakers, and discuss the habits of mind required to accomplish these tasks.

27. Ask students to investigate the significance of the school's traditions. Which traditions emphasize the habits of mind?

28. Place a premium on good sporting behavior in physical education and sports programs. How are competing honorably and habits of mind related? How does participation in sports contribute to good habits of mind in life beyond sports?

29. Interview students from several grade levels. Ask, "What does it take to be successful in this school?" Compare what they report with the list of habits of mind.

30. Regularly weave discussion of the habits of mind into history and literature classes.

31. Insist that accuracy and precision matter. Homework should be handed in on time—neat, complete, and accurate.

32. When forming cooperative learning groups, review the habits of mind. Ask groups to select one habit to become the focus of group work. Toward the end of the work time, stop and reflect on how this habit of mind affected the group members' interactions. Such reflection will also require group members to name indicators that they are using the habit of mind.

33. In literature discussions, ask questions that encourage reflecting on the habits of mind in the author's meaning, characters, beauty of the text, feelings the words produced, and applications of learnings to real-life situations.

34. Build habits of mind related to empathy by inviting students to put themselves in the shoes of the people they are reading about or studying in literature or social studies.

35. Read and discuss biographies from all subject areas. Help students identify the core or defining characteristics of each person studied. How do these characteristics compare with the habits of mind?

36. Invite students to write thoughtful letters that include explanations of how they use the habits of mind. Examples are thank-you notes, letters to public officials, and letters to the editor.

37. Assign homework that stimulates and challenges students to perform the habits of mind.

38. Set up a buddy reading system between an older and younger class. Teach the older students habits of mind that will make their teaching experience successful. Also teach the older students how to draw upon the habits of mind in interpreting a story and characters.

39. Ask students to memorize poetry and important prose, such as the Preamble to the Constitution or the Gettysburg Address. Have them translate the ideas in these works into habits of mind vocabulary. Ask them to reflect on why these works are worthy of memorization.

40. In science, explore the ethical considerations of a particular field of study. How do the habits of mind illuminate the moral side of science?

41. In math classes, specifically address habits such as taking responsible risks, persisting, and striving for accuracy. Why are these habits essential to understanding math? How are these habits applicable in other subject areas, in school, and in life?

42. In social studies, examine and reexamine the responsibilities of a citizen. What can students and staff do now to build the habits of mind of responsible citizenship?

43. Make classroom expectations of the habits of mind clear, and hold students accountable for meeting those expectations.

44. Give students sufficient and timely feedback about their work using the habits of mind terminology.

45. Invite students to "adopt an elder" from the community. Arrange for students to visit, write letters to, read to, and explain the habits of mind to their adoptee.

46. Invite graduates to return and talk about their experiences with the habits of mind. Ask them to discuss which habits can help make transitions successful: from elementary to middle school, from middle school to high school, or from high school to college or work.

47. During election years, encourage students to research candidates' positions, listen to debates, and participate in voter registration drives. Ask students to analyze the candidates' background and platform in terms of the habits of mind.

48. Organize a visit to a meeting of the city council, board of supervisors, board of education, or other public decision-making body. Beforehand, share with these groups that students have been learning the habits of mind, and that they want to look for the habits in action in the meetings.

49. Interview parents about how they use the habits of mind in their profession, job, or career. Which of the habits of mind make them successful in their work?

50. Have students shadow school personnel to look for use of the habits of mind.

51. Set up a school-to-career program with an expectation that students will learn about the use of habits of mind in the workplace.

52. In the computer lab, ask students to discuss the use of habits of mind as they are working with technology.

53. Place a sign in the playground that suggests students use the habits of mind when they are playing with one another.

54. Study television programs for examples of the habits of mind. Share this information with students, and ask them to do their own television study looking for the habits.

55. Select and watch movies to determine which habits of mind the main characters exemplify (e.g., *Babe* [listening with understanding and empathy]; *Chariots of Fire* [persisting]; *Saving Private Ryan* [taking responsible risks]; and *Apollo 13* [creating, imagining, innovating]).

56. Place signs in the library or media center supporting use of the habits of mind.

57. Study great painters and consider how the habits of mind might have influenced their work.

58. Set up a metacognitive journal for the whole class where students can record observations of the habits of mind.

59. Examine the pictures, icons, and heroes on the coins and currency from countries other than the United States. Discover why they qualify as national icons, and which of the habits of mind are exemplified in these people's lives.

60. Take advantage of school holidays (e.g., Presidents' Birthday, Martin Luther King Jr. Day, Labor Day, and Memorial Day) to explain why the habits of mind were important in the lives of those we celebrate.

61. Have a party for each habit. Make up place mats with a logo for the habit you are celebrating.

62. Role-play a student-led conference, and emphasize which habits students would use to describe their work.

63. Role-play a field trip, and emphasize which habits would be used on the trip.

64. Write a letter to the senior citizen group in your community. Ask them to describe how they used the habits when they were younger, as they progressed through their lives and careers, and at the present stage of their lives.

65. Tell students who your heroes or heroines are and why you chose them.

66. Hang pictures of heroes and heroines in classrooms and halls. Include brief biographies explaining how these exceptional people demonstrated the habits of mind.

67. Ask students to prepare a report on a living public figure ("My Personal Hero"). The report should focus on how this individual embodies the habits of mind.

68. Include a study of local heroes and heroines in social studies. What makes these people heroes, and how do they live out the habits of mind?

69. Celebrate the birthdays of heroes and heroines by discussing how the habits of mind contributed to their accomplishments.

70. Use morning announcements, school and classroom bulletin boards, and the school newsletter to highlight student and faculty accomplishments with the habits of mind.

71. Develop a bulletin board where teachers, administrators, and students can share awareness of, use of, and growth in the habits of mind.

72. Catch students being "intelligent," and celebrate their efforts.

73. Use a variety of communications to tell parents how their children are using the habits of mind: personal notes, phone calls, personal visits, and classroom newsletters.

74. Send a letter home to parents before the school year starts. Introduce yourself, your classroom, your enthusiasm, your expectations, and the habits of mind.

75. Use the school newsletter to keep parents informed about students' use of the habits of mind. Include anecdotes of commendable student performance.

76. Develop a list of suggested readings and resources related to the habits of mind. Share this resource with parents.

77. Include a "parents' corner" in the school newsletter where parents can share parenting tips, book titles, and homework helps that further the habits of mind.

78. During parent-teacher conferences, ask about parents' concerns. Model the habits of listening with understanding and empathy, and thinking and communicating with clarity and precision.

79. Invite managers and employees from industry and the corporate world to visit your school. Share with them the habits of mind. Ask them to explain how they encourage the habits of mind in their business.

80. Prepare a videotape program to show to parents, new teachers, and district personnel. This tape should describe the habits of mind and illustrate how they are cultivated in your school and classrooms.

81. Create bulletin boards that focus on student work, with an analysis of how the habits of mind informed the work.

82. Ask students to create a way to communicate the habits of mind at back-to-school night.

83. On a classroom wall, place large sheets of paper with magic markers attached to each. Put the name of each habit on a sheet. Ask parents to make associations—what comes to mind when they think of each habit—and write their associations on the papers.

84. Write a letter to businesses and corporations asking how they use the habits of mind.

85. Make a chart for the habits of mind. Use it to track the class's growth in using the habits of mind.

86. Interview community members to discover their perceptions about the habits of mind.

87. Provide bookmarks that have the habits of mind printed on them.

88. Make bumper stickers that celebrate the school's dedication to the habits of mind.

89. Have students develop their own buttons to hand out as a reward when someone uses the habits of mind.

90. Create plays, poems, and dialogues in which the habits of mind are pertinent.

91. In colonial times, children made samples with important mottoes and aphorisms. Create a needlepoint or cross-stitch project centered around the habits of mind.

92. Create a quilt using the habits of mind for the pieces.

93. Design plaques for the classroom with the habits of mind.

94. Create rap songs for the habits of mind.

95. _____

96. _____

97. _____

98. _____

99. _____

100. _____

101. _____

SELF-ASSESSING YOUR SCHOOL

ARTHUR L. COSTA AND BENA KALLICK

This appendix is a tool to help you assess your school's progress toward creating a learning culture grounded in the habits of mind. We have developed seven indicators to be evaluated using a framework for continuous improvement (see Chapter 1 for a more detailed explanation of this framework). The framework asks organizations to respond to three questions:

- What *approach* are we taking?
- Do what degree do we see *implementation*?
- What is the evidence of *results*?

The tool provides three levels to measure progress:

- *In the habit*. The behavior has become habituated throughout the organization. The behavior is a cultural norm and is performed spontaneously.
- *Practicing*. There are conscious and explicit procedures and strategies for focusing on, installing, and monitoring the behavior throughout the organization.
- *Aware*. There is an appreciation of the value of and an understanding of the need for the behavior.

Indicator 1: Shared Vision, Outcomes, and Goals. The school shows evidence of explicit statements about and graphic representations of the district's direction. The entire school community demonstrates clear communication about the habits of mind. Staff members focus on how students use the habits of mind to raise their levels of performance.

COMPONENTS OF SELF-ASSESSMENT

Level of Progress	Approach	Implementation	Results
In the Habit	The school has processes for building and revisiting the shared vision and goals based on analysis of student learning. The vision is clearly articulated and readily available.	All members of the school community help develop a vision. They may draft the vision or help revise it. Staff members feel a strong responsibility for implementing the goals.	The vision and goals are assessed as part of a continuous improvement plan. A significant measure of success is the degree to which the vision is realized in students' learning.
Practicing	The school has processes for developing a shared vision based on an analysis of student learning. Information about the vision and goals is available.	Some members of the school community help develop a vision. Staff members feel the beginning of a sense of responsibility for implementing the goals.	The board of education and the school staff assess the vision and goals. Measures of success are largely student focused.
Aware	The district sees the need to bring together a representative group to build a vision.	Community members, the board of education, teachers, administrators, and students begin to discuss a vision and goals.	The school community begins to tie the vision and goals to results of student learning.

86

Indicator 2: Curriculum, Instruction, and Assessment. The school's continuous redesign of curriculum and instruction specifically integrates the habits of mind. The school has a clear process for planning and implementing curriculum and instruction. These processes include reflecting on student work to see how well that work evidences use of the habits of mind. Curriculum designers use the habits of mind to ensure alignment among the shared vision, goals, and outcomes of the district.

COMPONENTS OF SELF-ASSESSMENT

Level of Progress	Approach	Implementation	Results
In the Habit	The school has a comprehensive process for the school community to continually examine and redesign curriculum and instruction based on performance of the habits of mind.	All members of the school community integrate and apply the habits of mind in their daily interactions.	Staff members can articulate significant improvements in student learning related to the habits of mind.
Practicing	The school has a process for the school community to begin to redesign curriculum and instruction based on performance of the habits of mind.	Some members of the school community integrate and apply the habits of mind in their daily interactions.	Staff members can articulate some improvements in student learning related to the habits of mind.
Aware	The school has identified a need for a comprehensive process for the school community to redesign curriculum and instruction based on the habits of mind.	A few staff members have participated in curriculum redesign based on integration of the habits of mind.	Interactions between students and teachers in some classrooms reflect the habits of mind.

Indicator 3: School Culture. The school is filled with an atmosphere of trust and respect, which is established through the habits of mind. Staff members have traditions to share new ideas and products that have been developed through using the habits of mind. Staff members also celebrate and reward work with the habits. There is visual and written evidence of using the habits. Staff members are loyal to change and innovation.

COMPONENTS OF SELF-ASSESSMENT

Level of Progress	Approach	Implementation	Results
In the Habit	The school has a comprehensive process for aligning vision and goals. The school uses a variety of methods to infuse the habits into the culture, such as prominently displayed visual and written artifacts, rewards and celebrations, and action research.	All members of the school community may be recognized for their use of the habits of mind. When an outsider comes to the school, an invitation to learn through the habits of mind is immediately apparent. Community members adopt innovations and experiments that have been successful.	Staff members see a significant increase in student learning related to the alignment with, commitment to, and loyalty toward the habits of mind. Successful innovations and experiments have been documented, and they demonstrate an improvement in student performance.
Practicing	The school is developing a process for aligning vision and goals with artifacts. The school has initiated a process for rewarding and celebrating the habits of mind. Innovation and experimentation are encouraged.	Some members of the school community are involved with rewards and celebrations. Participation in innovations and experiments has increased. Some staff members are using action research to document results.	Students are responding to the awards, recognition, and visible signs of the habits of mind. Performance is improving as a result of bringing the habits of mind to their attention. Innovations and experiments show the promise of increased student performance.
Aware	The school has identified a need for developing a process to make the habits of mind visible in the buildings. The school is searching for a way to honor the habits as a part of daily life. Diversity that leads to innovation and experimentation is beginning to develop.	Task groups are forming to develop a process for rewards, celebrations, and bringing the habits of mind to the attention of the whole community.	Staff and students are beginning to notice the habits of mind as they are discussed, and sometimes used, within the school community.

Indicator 4: Communication and Collaboration. The school has an established process for communicating and collaborating with parents, students, administrators, and teams. Reporting procedures show evidence of improved performance in the context of the habits of mind.

COMPONENTS OF SELF-ASSESSMENT

Level of Progress	Approach	Implementation	Results
In the Habit	The school has a comprehensive process for interactions with parents and other community members. The habits of mind serve as facilitating guidelines.	Meetings, teamwork, reports, and informal interactions reflect using the habits of mind.	The interconnectedness and involvement of all community members contribute to significant improvement in student learning over time.
Practicing	The school is developing a process for interactions with parents and other community members. The habits of mind serve as facilitating guidelines.	Some meetings and team groups are using the habits of mind as part of process observation. Informal interactions reflect a change in the degree of civility and respect for one another.	Students see the interconnectedness and involvement of school community members. As a result, the use of the habits of mind increases in their behaviors and work.
Aware	The school sees a need for establishing the habits of mind to guide effective communication among staff, students, and community. The school also sees a need to establish collaborative groups to work together on the habits of mind throughout the curriculum.	The school has begun to use newsletters and announcements to tell the community about the habits of mind. Groups and individuals are beginning to discuss the habits of mind.	Staff and students begin to talk about the habits of mind. Community and parents are informed of intentions and given descriptions of the habits of mind.

Indicator 5: Leadership. District leaders use the habits of mind for coaching, stewarding the change process, and structuring the environment. They strive to model using the habits of mind in all their work. Leadership is distributed among staff members, who also emerge as strong role models for using the habits of mind.

COMPONENTS OF SELF-ASSESSMENT

Level of Progress	Approach	Implementation	Results
In the Habit	The school has a systemic understanding of the need for process-oriented leadership skills and opportunities for planning such processes. A comprehensive system is in place for staff members to function in leadership roles.	People in leadership positions use strong facilitating processes for accomplishing work. There is a broad distribution of leadership among staff, students, and community members.	Staff members see a significant improvement in student learning related to the use of the habits of mind because of students' leadership roles and functions.
Practicing	The school is developing a process for understanding the need for process-oriented leadership. The staff is developing a plan to include a greater number of people in the community as leaders.	Some members of the leadership group use the facilitating processes for accomplishing work. More staff members, students, and community members are participating in leadership functions.	Staff members see an increase in student learning and empowerment related to the use of the habits of mind because of students' leadership roles and functions.
Aware	The school understands the need for distributed leadership. The school has also identified the need for a systematic plan for including the habits of mind as a facilitating structure for such change.	Staff members recognize a need for, and are prepared to set up, structures that foster a broader sense of leadership.	Students feel they can be a part of leading change needed in the school; they do not feel they are captive to adults' decisions.

Indicator 6: Resourceful School Community. The habits of mind mobilize the school community. The habits help staff members find imaginative ways to generate financial resources and to create and manage time.

COMPONENTS OF SELF-ASSESSMENT

Level of Progress	Approach	Implementation	Results
In the Habit	The school has a comprehensive process for generating, allocating, mobilizing, and coordinating resources such as energy, time, and money.	All program decisions are aligned with the vision and goals, and they include plans for generating resources to ensure achievement of results.	Staff members see a significant improvement in student learning based on carefully considered use of resources.
Practicing	The board of education, with the district leaders, has developed a process for generating needed school resources.	Some staff members make efforts to locate and generate human, financial, and material resources to achieve the vision and goals.	Staff members and students see an increasing sense of community ownership related to the use of precious resources.
Aware	The board of education and district leaders understand the need for resources.	Staff members are planning a process to generate resources. Allocation of resources is aligned with criteria for decision making.	Staff members see an increasing sense of creativity among colleagues as they struggle with limited resources.

Indicator 7: Continuous Learning. The habits of mind are a framework for continuous learning. The school systematically collects and analyzes data for self-evaluation and explores opportunities for new learning and growth. Staff members seek evidence of student learning in multiple forms and from multiple perspectives. Feedback spirals help guide their work.

COMPONENTS OF SELF-ASSESSMENT

Level of Progress	Approach	Implementation	Results
In the Habit	The school shows systematic, ongoing development of appropriate measures based on data gathering from a variety of sources.	The entire professional staff uses multiple forms of assessment measures.	Staff members see significant improvements in student learning by using multiple measures. Staff members self-assess regularly to modify their behavior and work.
Practicing	The school identifies new and varied forms of assessment. Teachers have opportunities to learn and share new techniques.	Most professional staff use multiple forms of assessment measures.	Staff members see systemic changes in student and teacher performance based on knowledge from assessment measures. They are beginning to use self-assessment as part of ongoing learning.
Aware	The school understands the feedback spiral as a concept of continuous growth.	Some staff members use a planning matrix to identify present practices within the system.	Staff members recognize needs to be addressed in the system.

BIBLIOGRAPHY

Following are books and articles that influenced our thinking as we prepared the Habits of Mind series.

Ames, J. E. (1997). *Mastery: Interviews with 30 remarkable people*. Portland, OR: Rudra Press.

Baron, J. B., & Sternberg, R. (Eds.). (1987). *Teaching thinking skills: Theory and practice*. New York: W. H. Freeman.

Bellanca, J., Costa, A., & Fogarty, R. (Eds.). (1991). *If minds matter: A foreword to the future* (Vols. 1 & 2). Palatine, IL: SkyLight Publishing, Inc.

Beyer, B. (1997). *Improving student thinking: A comprehensive approach*. Boston, MA: Allyn and Bacon.

Brown, J. L. (1995). *Observing Dimensions of Learning in classrooms and schools*. Alexandria, VA: Association for Supervision and Curriculum Development.

Caine, R. N., & Caine, G. (1997). *Education on the edge of possibility*. Alexandria, VA: Association for Supervision and Curriculum Development.

Caine, R. N., & Caine, G. (1997). *Unleashing the power of perceptual change: The potential of brain-based teaching*. Alexandria, VA: Association for Supervision and Curriculum Development.

Coles, R. (1997). *The moral intelligence of children*. New York: Random House.

Costa, A. (Ed.). (1991). *Developing minds: A resource book for teaching thinking* (Rev. ed., Vol. 1). Alexandria, VA: Association for Supervision and Curriculum Development.

Costa, A. (1991). *The school as a home for the mind*. Arlington Heights, IL: SkyLight Publishing, Inc.

Costa, A., & Garmston, R. (1994). *Cognitive coaching: A foundation for renaissance schools*. Norwood, MA: Christopher-Gordon Publishers.

Costa, A., & Garmston, R. (1998, October). Five human passions. *Think: The Magazine on Critical and Creative Thinking*, 14–17.

Costa, A., & Kallick, B. (1995). *Assessment in the learning organization: Shifting the paradigm*. Alexandria, VA: Association for Supervision and Curriculum Development.

Costa, A., & Liebmann, R. (Eds.). (1997). *Envisioning process as content: Toward a renaissance curriculum*. Thousand Oaks, CA: Corwin Press.

Costa, A., & Liebmann, R. (Eds.). (1997). *Supporting the spirit of learning: When process is content*. Thousand Oaks, CA: Corwin Press.

Costa, A., & Liebmann, R. (Eds.). (1997). *The process-centered schools: Sustaining a renaissance community*. Thousand Oaks, CA: Corwin Press.

Costa, A., & Lowery, L. (1989). *Techniques for teaching thinking*. Pacific Grove, CA: Critical Thinking Press and Software.

Covey, S. (1989). *The seven habits of highly effective people: Restoring the character ethic*. New York: Simon & Schuster.

Damasio, A. R. (1994). *Descartes' error: Emotion, reason, and the human brain*. New York: G. P. Putnam and Sons.

de Bono, E. (1986). *Six thinking hats*. New York: Viking.

de Bono, E. (1991). The CoRT thinking program. In A. Costa (Ed.), *Developing minds: Programs for teaching thinking* (Rev. ed., Vol. 2, pp. 27–32). Alexandria, VA: Association for Supervision and Curriculum Development.

Diamond, M., & Hopson, J. (1998). *Magic trees of the mind: How to nurture your child's intelligence, creativity, and healthy emotions from birth through adolescence*. New York: Penguin Putnam.

Dyer, J. (1997). Humor as process. In A. Costa & R. Liebmann (Eds.), *Envisioning process as content: Toward a renaissance curriculum*. Thousand Oaks, CA: Corwin Press.

Ennis, R. (1991). Goals for a critical thinking curriculum. In A. Costa (Ed.), *Developing minds: A resource book for teaching thinking* (Rev. ed., Vol. 1, pp. 68–71). Alexandria, VA: Association for Supervision and Curriculum Development.

Faccioni, P. A., & Facione, N. C. (1992). *The California critical thinking dispositions inventory*. Milbrae, CA: The California Academic Press.

Feuerstein, R. (1980). *Instrumental enrichment: An intervention program for cognitive modifiability*. Baltimore: University Park Press.

Fogarty, R. (1998). *Brain-Compatible classrooms*. Arlington Heights, IL: SkyLight Publishing, Inc.

Fullan, M. G. (1993). *Change forces: Probing the depth of educational reform.* New York: Falmer Press.

Fullan, M. G., & Stiegelbauer, S. (1991). *The new meaning of educational change* (2nd ed.). New York: Teachers College Press.

Gardner, H. (1983). *Frames of mind: The theory of multiple intelligences.* New York: BasicBooks.

Gardner, H. (1993). *Multiple intelligences: The theory in practice.* New York: BasicBooks.

Gardner, H. (1999). *The disciplined mind: What all students should understand.* New York: Simon and Schuster.

Garmston, R. J., & Wellman, B. M. (1999). *The adaptive school: A sourcebook for developing collaborative groups.* Norwood, MA: Christopher-Gordon Publishers.

Glatthorn, A., & Baron, J. (1991). The good thinker. In A. Costa (Ed.), *Developing minds: A resource book for teaching thinking* (Rev. ed., Vol. 1, pp. 63–67). Alexandria, VA: Association for Supervision and Curriculum Development.

Gould, S. J. (1981). *The mismeasure of man.* New York: Norton.

Guilford, J. P. (1967). *The nature of human intelligence.* New York: McGraw-Hill.

Hargreave, A. (1997). Rethinking educational change: Going deeper and wider in the quest for success. In A. Hargreave (Ed.), *Rethinking educational change with heart and mind* (1997 ASCD Yearbook). Alexandria VA: Association for Supervision and Curriculum Development.

Kotulak, R. (1997). *Inside the brain: Revolutionary discoveries of how the mind works.* Kansas City, MO: Andrews and McMeel.

Lipman, M., Sharp, A., & Oscanyan, F. (1980). *Philosophy in the classroom.* Philadelphia: Temple University Press.

Lipton, L., & Wellman, B. (1999). *Pathways to understanding: Patterns and practices in the learning-focused classroom.* Guilford, VT: Pathways Publishing.

Lochhead, J. (2000). *Thinkback: A user's guide to minding the mind.* Hillsdale, NJ: Lawrence Erlbaum.

Lowery, L. (1998, November). How new science curriculums reflect brain research. *Educational Leadership, 56*(3), 26–30.

Machado, L. A. (1980). *The right to be intelligent* (M. C. Wheeler, Trans.). New York: Pergamon Press.

Marzano, R. J. (1992). *Implementing Dimensions of Learning.* Alexandria, VA: Association for Supervision and Curriculum Development.

Marzano, R. J. (1997). *Dimensions of Learning* (2nd ed.). Alexandria, VA: Association for Supervision and Curriculum Development.

Marzano, R. J., Pickering, D., & McTighe, J. (1994). *Assessing student outcomes: Performance assessment using the Dimensions of Learning model.* Alexandria, VA: Association for Supervision and Curriculum Development.

Parry, T., & Gregory, G. (1998). *Designing brain-compatible learning.* Arlington Heights, IL: SkyLight Publishing, Inc.

Perkins, D. (1981). *The mind's best work.* Cambridge, MA: Harvard University Press.

Perkins, D. (1986). *Knowledge as design.* Hillsdale, NJ: Erlbaum.

Perkins, D. (1991). What creative thinking is. In A. Costa (Ed.), *Developing minds: A resource book for teaching thinking* (Rev. ed., Vol. 1, pp. 85–88). Alexandria, VA: Association for Supervision and Curriculum Development.

Perkins, D. (1992). *Smart schools: From training memories to educating minds.* New York: Free Press.

Perkins, D. (1995). *Outsmarting IQ: The emerging science of learnable intelligence.* New York: Free Press.

Perkins, D., Goodrich, H., Tishman, S., & Owen, J. (1993). *Thinking connections: Learning to think and thinking to learn.* Menlo Park, CA: Addison-Wesley Publishing Company.

Presseissen, B. (Ed.) (1999). *Teaching for intelligence: A collection of articles* (Vol. 1). Arlington Heights, IL: SkyLight Publishing, Inc.

Resnick, L., & Hall, M. (1998, Fall). Learning organizations for sustainable education reform. *Daedalus: Journal of the American Academy of Arts and Sciences,* 89–118.

Senge, P. (1990). *The fifth discipline: The art and practice of the learning organization.* New York: Doubleday/Currency.

Senge, P., Ross, R., Smith, B., Roberts, C., & Kleiner, A. (1994). *The fifth discipline fieldbook: A fieldbook for teachers, administrators, parents, and everyone who cares about education.* New York: Doubleday/Currency.

Sternberg, R. (1983). *How can we teach intelligence?* Philadelphia: Research for Better Schools.

Sternberg, R. (1985). *Beyond IQ: A triarchic theory of human intelligence.* Cambridge: Cambridge University Press.

Sternberg, R., Torff, B., & Grigorenko, E. (1998). Teaching for successful intelligence raises school achievement. *Phi Delta Kappan, 79*(9), 667–669.

Sternberg, R., & Wagner, R. K. (Eds.). (1986). *Practical intelligence: Nature and origins of competence in the everyday world.* Cambridge: Cambridge University Press.

Swartz, R., Fischer, S. D., & Parks, S. (1999). *Infusing the teaching of critical and creative thinking into secondary science: A lesson design handbook.* Pacific Grove, CA: Critical Thinking Press and Software.

Swartz, R., & Parks, S. (1994). *Infusing the teaching of critical and creative thinking into content instruction: A lesson design handbook for the elementary grades.* Pacific Grove, CA: Critical Thinking Press and Software.

Tishman, S., Perkins, D., & Jay, E. (1995). *The thinking classroom: Learning and teaching in a culture of thinking.* Boston: Allyn and Bacon.

Waldrop, M. M. (1992). *Complexity: The emerging science at the edge of order and chaos.* New York: Simon & Schuster.

Whimbey, A., & Lochhead, J. (1999). *Problem solving and comprehension.* Hillsdale, NJ: Erlbaum.

Whimbey, A., & Whimbey, L. (1975). *Intelligence can be taught.* New York: Dutton.

Wiggins, G., & McTighe, J. (1998). *Understanding by design.* Alexandria, VA: Association for Supervision and Curriculum Development.

Wolfe, P., & Brandt, R. (1998, November). What do we know from brain research? *Educational Leadership, 56*(3), 8–13.

Zuboff, S. (1988). *In the age of the smart machine: The future of work and power.* New York: BasicBooks.

ACKNOWLEDGMENTS

We wish to express our appreciation to the many contributors to this series of books. The descriptions of their experiences, lessons, implementation strategies, vignettes, and artwork are what give meaning, expression, and practicality to the habits of mind. To them we are eternally grateful.

We wish to thank John O'Neil, Nancy Modrak, Julie Houtz, Margaret Oosterman, and other members of the ASCD editorial staff who encouraged and guided us throughout this project. Our gratitude is expressed to our editor, René Bahrenfuss, for her flexibility, her striving for accuracy, and her persistence. We are appreciative of the artistic talents of Georgia McDonald and other ASCD design staff for the habits of mind icons. Without their attention to detail, striving for perfection, and creative imagination, this series could not have come to fruition.

We also wish to thank our assistants, Kim Welborn and Carol Hunsicker, whose secretarial skills and computer wizardry behind the scenes kept us organized and in communication with each other and with all the authors.

We pay particular tribute to Bena's husband, Charles, and Art's wife, Nancy, who tolerated our time away from them. Their love, encouragement, and understanding provided the support base for our success.

Finally, we wish to acknowledge the many teachers, administrators, and parents in the numerous schools and communities throughout the United States and abroad who have adopted and implemented the habits of mind and have found them a meaningful way to organize learning. The future world will be a more thoughtful, compassionate, and cooperative place because of their dedication to cultivating the habits of mind in students and modeling them in their own behavior.

TEACHER, SCHOOL, AND DISTRICT ACKNOWLEDGMENTS

We would like to thank the many teachers, schools, and districts throughout the United States and other countries who contributed to the writing of this book. Their combined efforts helped us develop a comprehensive presentation of the 16 habits of mind.

California
Renee Affolter and Frank J.
  Jacques
Sir Francis Drake High School
San Anselmo, California

Encinal High School
Alameda, California

Hawaii
Angie Chock
Royal Elementary School
Honolulu, Hawaii

Maryland
Friendship Valley Elementary
  School
Westminster, Maryland

Minnesota
Donna Norton Swindal
Hidden Valley Elementary School
Edward N. Neill Elementary
  School
Burnsville, Minnesota

New Jersey
Cherry Hill West High School
Cherry Hill, New Jersey

New York
Mamaroneck Avenue School
Mamaroneck, New York

Rick Wilhelm
West Orchard Elementary School
Chappaqua, New York

New Zealand
Alan Cooper
St. George's School
Wanganui, New Zealand

Texas
Stephen Gasken
Danbury High School
Danbury, Texas

Oregon
John Kiemele
Raleigh Hills Elementary School
Beaverton, Oregon

Virginia
Fred Morton
Montgomery County, Virginia

Wisconsin
Three agencies in Eau Claire:
• Eau Claire Area School District, represented by Laurie Hittman, executive director of instructional services and chair of the Eau Claire District Critical Thinking Leadership Team.
• Meadowview Elementary School, represented by the Critical Thinking Leadership Team: Ilene Doty, principal; Gerry Holt, teacher; Mary Kay Kopf, teacher; Karen Hirsch, resource teacher; and Laurie Hittman (executive director of instructional services, Eau Claire Area School District).
• DeLong Middle School, represented by Deborah Hansen, coordinator of staff development.

INDEX

Note: An *f* after a page number indicates a reference to a figure. An entry in bold-face refers to one of the 16 habits of mind.

ABOUT THE AUTHORS

Arthur L. Costa is an emeritus professor of education at California State University, Sacramento, and codirector of the Institute for Intelligent Behavior in Cameron Park, California. He has been a classroom teacher, a curriculum consultant, and an assistant superintendent for instruction, as well as the director of educational programs for the National Aeronautics and Space Administration. He has made presentations and conducted workshops in all 50 states, as well as in Mexico, Central and South America, Canada, Australia, New Zealand, Africa, Europe, Asia, and the Islands of the South Pacific.

Costa has written numerous articles and books, including *Techniques for Teaching Thinking* (with Larry Lowery), *The School as a Home for the Mind*, and *Cognitive Coaching: A Foundation for Renaissance Schools* (with Robert Garmston). He is editor of *Developing Minds: A Resource Book for Teaching Thinking* and coeditor (with Rosemarie Liebmann) of the Process as Content Trilogy: *Envisioning Process as Content, Supporting the Spirit of Learning*, and *The Process-Centered School.*

Active in many professional organizations, Costa served as president of the California Association for Supervision and Curriculum Development and as national president of the Association for Supervision and Curriculum Development, 1988–89. Costa can be reached at Search Models Unlimited, P.O. Box 362, Davis, CA 95617-0362; phone/fax: 530-756-7872; e-mail: artcosta@aol.com.

Bena Kallick is a private consultant providing services to school districts, state departments of education, professional organizations, and public agencies throughout the United States and internationally. Kallick received her doctorate in educational evaluation at Union Graduate School. Her areas of focus include group dynamics, creative and critical thinking, and alternative assessment strategies in the classroom. Her written work includes *Literature to Think About* (a whole language curriculum published with Weston Woods Studios), *Changing Schools into Communities for Thinking*, and *Assessment in the Learning Organization* (coauthored with Arthur Costa).

Formerly a teachers' center director, Kallick also created a children's museum based on problem solving and invention. She was the coordinator of a high school alternative designed for at-risk students. She is cofounder of Technology Pathways, a company designed to provide easy-to-use software that helps integrate and make sense of data from curriculum, instruction, and assessment. Kallick's teaching appointments have included Yale University School of Organization and Management, University of Massachusetts Center for Creative and Critical Thinking, and Union Graduate School. She was previously on the board of the Apple Foundation and is presently on the board of Jobs for the Future. Kallick can be reached at 12 Crooked Mile Rd., Westport, CT 06880; phone/fax: 203-227-7261; e-mail: bkallick@aol.com.

Deborah Hansen is an associate principal at DeLong Middle School in Eau Claire, Wisconsin. She has also been a social worker, school counselor, and staff development facilitator. She served as an adjunct faculty member at the University of Wisconsin in Eau Claire for six years, working with the teacher education program. She has been active in adult learning and focused her dissertation on adult learning, staff development, career stages, and job satisfaction. Hansen serves on the board of directors of the Wisconsin Association for Supervision and Curriculum Development. She is chair of the communications committee and writes articles for their publication, *Highlighter*. Hansen can be reached at DeLong Middle School, 2000 Vine St., Eau Claire, WI 54703; phone: 715-839-6293; fax: 715-838-2616; e-mail: dhansen@ecasd.k12.wi.us.

David Perkins, codirector of Harvard Project Zero, is a senior research associate at the Harvard Graduate School of Education. He is the author of several books, including *Smart Schools: From Training Memories to Educating Minds* and *Outsmarting IQ: The Emerging Science of Learnable Intelligence*, and many articles. He has helped develop instructional programs and approaches for teaching understanding and thinking, including initiatives in South Africa, Israel, and Latin America. He is a former Guggenheim Fellow. Perkins can be reached at Project Zero, Harvard Graduate School of Education, 323 Longfellow Hall, 13 Appian Way, Cambridge, MA 02138; phone: 617-495-4342; fax: 617-496-4288; e-mail: David_Perkins@pz.harvard.edu.